# IF IN TIME

# IF IN TIME

## Selected Poems
### 1975–2000

## ANN LAUTERBACH

PENGUIN POETS

PENGUIN BOOKS
Published by the Penguin Group
Penguin Putnam Inc., 375 Hudson Street,
New York, New York 10014, U.S.A.
Penguin Books Ltd, 27 Wrights Lane,
London W8 5TZ, England
Penguin Books Australia Ltd, Ringwood,
Victoria, Australia
Penguin Books Canada Ltd, 10 Alcorn Avenue,
Toronto, Ontario, Canada M4V 3B2
Penguin Books (N.Z.) Ltd, 182-190 Wairau Road,
Auckland 10, New Zealand

Penguin Books Ltd, Registered Offices:
Harmondsworth, Middlesex, England

First published in Penguin Books 2001

1   3   5   7   9   10   8   6   4   2

Page ix constitutes an extension of this copyright page.

Selections from Ann Lauterbach's *Clamour, And For Example*, and *On a Stair* are
reprinted by permission of Penguin Books, a member of Penguin Putnam Inc.
Copyright © Ann Lauterbach, 1991, 1994, 1997.

CIP Data available
ISBN 0-14-058930-9

Printed in the United States of America
Set in Bembo
Designed by Suvi Asch

*To John Ashbery, Kenward Elmslie, Barbara Guest*

# ACKNOWLEDGMENTS

Many persons have given support over the years to this work. I want to thank, in particular, Nan Graham, Peter and Susan Straub, Diana Michener, Jeannette Watson, Bradford Morrow, Stacy Davis, Joan Richardson, Charles Altieri, and, for their assistance, Heather Ramsdell and Camille Guthrie. To TSJ—the gift.

Special thanks to Paul Slovak at Viking Penguin.

Some of the poems in the first section have been published, often in earlier drafts. The author gratefully acknowledges the editors and journals in which they first appeared.

"September Song," "Typography," "Diorama of the Uninhabited Yes," "Walk," "Legacy," "New Brooms" supported in part by a grant from the Marion Center, College of Santa Fe, for the project National Millennium Survey; "Walk" published in *Countermeasures* 11. "Winter Strawberries," "Narcolepsy," "Frayed Edges," "Splendor" in *Conjunctions*.

For permission to publish poems from *Before Recollection* (Princeton University Press, 1987) the author gratefully acknowledges the Princeton University Press.

*Many Times, But Then* was published by the University of Texas Press in 1979 in the Poetry Series (no. 4), Iris Hill, editor.

*That this is I,*
*Not mine, which wakes*
*To where the present*
*Sun pours in the present, to the air perhaps*
*Of love and of*
*Conviction.*

——GEORGE OPPEN

*Time dissipates to shining ether the solid angularity of facts. No anchor, no cable, no fences, avail to keep a fact a fact.*

——RALPH WALDO EMERSON

# CONTENTS

## *from* MANY TIMES, BUT THEN *(1979)*

# IF IN TIME

# THE CALL

*Poems 1997-2000*

# TEMPLATE

An exhausted prostitute sits on a white puritanical bed
small in her dress, her eyes orientally sad.
In the window, the green light
of a pond gives order to the universe
although the male child, nine, asks
*what is that?* Knowing
bed, dress, sad, window, green and light,
having some notion of the pond,
not inquisitive about the universe because he
knows that too (it is where he is)
what he asks
of the scene is the doll.

A garden is an idea.
It is not plants flourishing in good soil,
not the edible dream, not
mildew in the cusps of mulch, not
Celtic glory—Cornwall, the Isle of Man,
the Ulster ballads

                   sad tunes
of the blue-eyed musician

      (the sky keeps returning to the pond

                (when I was a girl, there was

     a garden

     there were steps
     these steps went down

into magic
as in a story

where what is is
changed by language)

singing *a garden is an idea.*

      And the soloist's avidity, her song
before the morning din: trucks, warplanes, pickaxe,
churning air into lament and dust, as if waking
into the final cause

                the soloist, transcribing

these findings, is
puerile without history which is
also an idea.

*to Henry GC, later*

# SEPTEMBER SONG

But we           cantilevered
across the ruins
                    love in Lagos   Hollywood
                            but we
        photographed radiant
        in suits
                    but we
                clasping the bright entitlement of things

Illusion of quilts, including the barn door and the rake
to the extent that birds are outside, and all the tricks of film—
magic of space caught as dots, two
installed as particulars close to each other, their intimacy
achieved by the practice of something manipulated
so that it is almost, but not quite, real.

                    *To work quietly, seriously, productively*
                            *yellow hinges*
                        *isolated from drift*
                                *companions in patience, lost*
                                        *in the stars.*

The virulence of the age surrounded a small thicket of romance.
The people, bagged in rain,
fell up and up
into the basket-weave sky.
Somewhat like this, the mechanism of the day
thwarted our progress, so we spilled out
bereft of purpose. Fist of red leaves; a mild gray wind.
These old-fashioned contingencies shamed us
but the new had no agenda, no secret plan or past.
A young girl traveled swiftly over long grass into the inquisitive mode:
*Have you got a television? Where are your children?*
She seemed to understand the value of fruition
and the cost of abstention. Cartooned in the distance
she ran as fast as she could, hands crowded
with coins borrowed for keeps.

The old enemies
began to encroach, even as we sat on a roof
across from the crenellated tower
and watched a toy ball
fall into a drain as the day
swerved up a brick wall into night's dump.

# TYPOGRAPHY

Stalled at a lectern, a habit or price.
Snow fill and blur and the sidelong currents
from no direction, the direction of news
spun into an appeal
for the evident to withstand the friction of use.
The incentive of a backward glance
improvised the hour so as not to punish
its advent, in which a child first emerges
and a woman makes a reservation on a train.
These pop from the calendar like songs.
The girl in pearly shoes
knows to please
                    which is how
she begins to move
in the atmosphere of the heaping snow
among discontinued genes anonymously strewn.
Things she can and cannot do.
The scheme pulls apart
but nothing spills
except an arsenal of thinnest lines
on an unopened note, fluid
below the fledgling ice, not yet wholly dissolved.
Certain acuities float slowly off the bridge.
These she calls *derision flare, reflected apex,*
*ninth plunder,* depending on the wind, its correction as fate.
But nobody, in the sapphire spray, notices.
What are we to call the thing
that pulses along but does not connect, a
mute heart? And what about the person
who is guided away from us, what to call her?
Snow ruins the echo of its fall. You cannot hear
the small dust or liquid elicited,
near as can be, along the eyelid of time.
How pretty she looks under the covers
while stamina fails. Stamina is this world plus another.

*to Priscilla*

7

# DIORAMA OF THE UNINHABITED YES

And here, an exaggerated arc
—see
how its grin exceeds the joke—
and the featherweight drama

                                            liability of the newly wet
                        swelling the planks

The list, old among numbers, could be *six, seven,*
among these it could be
ideology skulking at the corner of an age
star-struck, emulating, singing along with the tune
*that smell of sweet perfume*

                            among numbers, filtered into the humid
                                high summer air
                  mouth open, lips in sync,
and the question comes up
dropped into the street below—

It could be Caravaggio
or the fleshy belief he inscribed,
dense filiation of desire, and so
a mythic arrangement is in order here, among these numbers,
a story decision on the back lot. So he comes toward her and says

*would you have a look at this script?*
*could you cut my hair?*
*would you mind lowering the shade?*

The answer   The direction of the first bed   The task

And now look, far
is near, next door is another century
whose shape reconfigures the topography of care.
It seems possible to notice a harem
gathering around the stump, wearing boas
and slacks, whispering into the dust.
Shall we address their dilemma?

The anticipated part is only part of the assignment,
part two is the repeated motif of law.
The nurse said *be prepared, strip.*
And we thought, given this premise, that she had seen
the thing slain and the unshared part dealt out among strangers,
those in the park, those in a boat, a few wandering across a bridge.
But this never happens in the city,
only usual begetting as the slant bends into a curl,
the curl a parenthetical remark or eyelash on the pillow of dawn.
Riots in the capital.
Europe destroyed under its canopy of culture.
This moves across the threshold into that
because the wind's fitful economy
parts only debris, laying claim to the moment
as if it were a lucky number pulled from a hat.

# WALK

Mistakenly on the other side's side: walking along.
Thinking this must be change, this discomfort.
Walking as on an island, the mausoleum across the yard.
Thus: a span, uncluttered, available: the dark.
The dark yard's discomfort, the breeze withheld.
Picturing and then being the picture, the still.
A red tugboat trolling, near the dam.
The dramatist walking by the taxi. No one waves.
Here we accumulate. One, two, among.

There were, of course, too many stories yoked to the original, too many
collisions under the scaffold. What we thought about seeped back under
the foundation, to become itself a kind of mud, luminous at night, during
the quiet night ride. We were in the uncomfortable stage, the eighth
month, its enormity a kind of pathos, the garden bloated beyond en-
chantment. Over there, across the bridge, another group gathered, spying
on the generations, summing them up. Right, they attested, sure enough.
Nobody had time to vote, and those that did, did for reasons only the
Op-Ed understood.

They were testing our right to continue.
We pretended to know.

But then there was the uncontaminated filigree of skin, youthful through
an extra pair of glasses, classically wide-eyed, the world as yet undimin-
ished by the burden of its authors. That old hymn, remember? Among the
disenfranchised nothing stirred, and the silt went easily over the new spill-
way, and the moon extended her rights of passage down into the arroyo.

Not belonging was a kind of errancy, a bluff seen by others as
refusal without implications.

In the room there were small movable tables.
In the room there was a pair of shoes.
In the room there was a book on the floor.
In the room certain things were missing.
In the room there were no mirrors.

The radio's episodic dial.
Bourgeois affinities of the newly polished leather.
The writer-in-exile speaks candidly to the reporter, eating nuts.
Modernism ends.
In the room music went on.
In the room a table was replaced; it was not a museum.
A flag fell across a stamp.
Unpleasant expenditures, body odors, tears.
New regulations undoing privacy.

Saturday. Lake Committee meeting.
Call from Martin.
Second call from Martin, no number.
Joan's scent in the hallway.
Rick's unhappiness with what he wrote.
Second book received *with compliments of the author* on a printed card.
Torrential rain.
First parking ticket.
Call from David.
Call from another David.
Call from Thomas. Full moon.
Small yellow pill. Small red pill.
Note from Elaine mentioning J. Crew.
Refusal to stay in room 205.
Aggressive male child in the park.
Mary Ann quotes René Char.
Idea of Prose.
George and Mary sailing. Sincerity and sailing, a remark.
Lilacs.
Lost Wax. Cookery.
Genius as economy without waste.
Pictures without captions.
Pictures of persons without names.

To excerpt the ordinary from splendor, the affluent cloister,
trapped in a small luminous box
in which everyone knows everyone else.
Could drop some names from the glossary,
delete a few consummations while
dressed in fatigues, the fatigue of need, the accepted norm,

sorrow and reality, the loved person dying, the leaves
lapsed, drawn forward
with autumn's litany of perishables:
book bags, shirts without monograms,
the if-then date.
Is it wise to abstain?
Such is the city's grail
that the hum is expansive, shorn
from prevailing silence and entrails of light.
Crave thee this dialogue? This touch?
Is an allegory of—
Let's walk a little into it.
David says that generation had something we lack,
*a calm mind.* David says
*perhaps only those from another country*
*can combine the rhetoric of feeling with*

I have forgotten the rest.

# LEGACY

1.

I am thinking again of drab
fly cycles
roof mumbling harmony
up in attics beyond deliberation I am
stunned (young man, you
have ruined this phase (I am thinking
the window is rotted and the flies are crafting their music
under a single nude (seen
thither and yon
in as many particulars:
the alert dust, the carefree bonanza
of a city (waiting in the dark
by the side of everything
paused under a shaft
little pool of blood on the curb
pink discrepancy of what we imagined
was terror: then
going on into the hills beyond the mall's crude angles
road stretched
counting the characters
not yet proven, not sold, not released
into what we had seen: old visitor, hawk,
I am waving good-bye.

2.

Shadow range
ekphrastic renovation of a spoon

without shelter
the thing delighted is kept

to follow the once
that, once said, was

inscribed on the tongue
to ask from the margin

will you come
to the incident's call

open the blinds
spill sun in his mouth

hope's flagrant shine
cast back to its arbor

stain on the dress
new twenty-dollar bill

malleable space
on a page of trials

clairvoyant current
under the paved

clues to the meaning
in the feathers of slang

passing a note
from fever to ash

3.

Yes and here

distributed as acronyms for praise, small

attributes

here

all along the way, as if marshaled,
testimony calibrated under the horn
so that we had seen in a leaf the Spartan vagary of time,
its credentials,
                              here
lasting under the last

permission sought, its style
coming around

as a decision to stay
one or three days
                    here
not as the recuperating genius of an age
not as the swooning female
not as the hieroglyph bomb

but ask who is here, who speaking—
Mr. Predictable Rage & Ms. Predictable Doubt
dance the Predictable Rag.

4.

Excessive and volatile, from which all detail is omitted.
Film me in costume. I want to be a soldier.
We went to the local store in search of thread.
That is all I recall of childhood.

# NEW BROOMS

Of representation *(frame)*
from one to another *(use)*
between the articulation *(space)*
of language *(tree)*
of clarity by means of *(intent)*
of humans *(speech)*
on the contrary *(response)*
with itself, in its own density *(earth)*
for it is not *(image)*
from the first to the second *(wave)*
seizes upon *(law)*
within the other *(us)*
without those of *(tradition)*
point by point *(nature)*
of or to *(the same)*

and so on into a possible good
the waxed carnation's cribbed flounce
shade distinctly wound among new brooms
panache of the ever-tan September

          And so what is said       is at an angle

architectural

      over the floor from which the soliloquy drafts
         upwards, as if restitution
           could be a chant surrounding disaster.

Bruise on the arm lingers in absentia.
Buzz saw in the alley.

Speech, oracle of intention, dissolves
into the sea's remission
as up through an imperfect net comes another exaltation.

2.

Some here twitch along a heading, out
out, and came thou back along the periphery,
shroud tracked, foregathered,
tune integrating chorale
tautly drawn into rainspit, down
through the breaking mirror's reminiscent shield, *bethou*
said the maiden, *bethou* said the monk.
*Not yet,* said the bird, elongating distance,
high among pines and pale rock.
But had we spoken of the quarry?
Or were we in a room, video-taped, among dry towels
and the humid inquisition of the crowd?
We were in the crowd, *"you and I" "he and she"* and so
transpired over its edge into
bodily harm: an eye for a hand, some mantra of war.
The stipulating crew began to assert its origins
and what pale and what golden
shimmied into paradox, whittling the streets with monograms,
the walls with cool but generative dust.
The pictures came back from their instants.
*A genetic stroke of luck is not to have this receptor*
Yet another instruction, one we still cannot read.

*to Thomas Dumm*

# WINTER STRAWBERRIES

You will find I have been guided by fate's
whispering tabernacle, into which
a cradle rocks the library's gold façade.
In dreamland, a word
is stuffed into a bag, the flight comes,
and what was promised
and what said
vanishes into the jet stream. Humor
is in my left shoe, damage control in the right,
my garb is a robe
woven into the nick of time.
But the dilemma under the passage
splits air's permissions and clones.
The long line to the altar
turns away, banyan trees
root on a sacred pile.
King Rat and Bird Flu scrabble the dust for clues.

Expertise of the antiquarian flirt.
Wishes something manual would happen.
A dusty limbo, plastic covered,
unevenly veiled despite the sky's arrest.

        *Not air,* said the clairvoyant,
*just particulars with space intervened.*
Whose fatigue cut into this robe?
Whose damage control?
*Clip, clip, clip,* hails from porcelain clouds,
an Orphic residue mimics the arcade.
Some isolated notes align stamina to trust, their
cause moving along, stubbornly annealed.

# NARCOLEPSY

Comes sarcastic November in mummy garb, hauling
*same old same old* what laid bare
what totaled. Sees thru the estimated costs, stench
collisions, inanimate dregs, remembers
the bruised figures, their
numerology as stars. *Up up, down down*
is how she counts as the hunters begin to hunt.

This is the plot of erasure, this the lavender bath.
Truth be known, the dark won by a landslide.

Yet friends in far January
await news of the front, cycling up the snow-clad hills.
They are to be exhumed from the grail of the keeper,
he who heralds what's here. To them, send dreams
that pop open when breathed on
and ask them to complete this sentence:
*If God is in the details, then . . .*

But in the end there was only a chair covered in velvet
and the sibling, dark as a forest, turned into words.
There were the stamps with monsters
and the stamps with flowers,
there was a dumpster of old paint.
Even the egalitarian whimsy of the gold rush
is in partial view: harbor's sleek hulls,
willow disintegrating in drapery and nonce.
What others did
taking us to task in the field, into archival maps
along a bank. What is it they wanted?
Among strangers, beyond the stamina of pictures
—the dancer on stage, his ruined feet,

        *as they would flail crops*
   *when the spring comes, and flood, and tassels*
          *rise, as my head—*

Across the ballast's drab plaster
a colder moment assumes shape.
And Thee, found inside eternity's crawl space,
midget doctrine of reckless variety,
homing pigeon of whatever returns,
what is your method now and
how do you know when it is finished?
When it detaches, when it comes to life at the edge of time.

# THE CALL

Had relinquished the moist tether, arguing
the curtains are spoiled
the car phone calling thru new dark
world scanned into humidity
racing under the floor in torrents

speculation on elements
(see! the moth matches the decor)

The call      how it made the roof play upward, out
from the skull's itinerary
                              sky-heaved, exposed
so that the grass meandered
and the relics
blown from the lips of the sea
                              inscribed
                                        *the inscription* we would say
calligraphy of the dome
of the unknown ceiling
cusp sewn into moorings at dawn
morphic residue
                    holding the soul in his arms
                                        rapt finger, instruction in stone
                                        passage of the wise, event undisclosed.

What is this dust leaking through a box at the king's knees?
What is this disastrous blue? A flower thinking? The sky reformed?
Can we step through the concatenation of hours, the will frozen and
importuned with objects—dismal Newton with his fingers engaged.
Flags edge down from their shelter, floating.
He has decided to exile the angels, their
false presentation of what comes next.
The gun, however, is prologue to a gun.
Sitting at lunch with the master, napkin folded
over the uneasy patois of remembrance, the exhibition
sparkling into the gray winter day, painted skull
flattened, flung out into an exactly exaggerated orbit.

In one window, when the curtains are pulled apart,
*everything* can be read, as if thru tears
a beloved face. In the other, a cardinal's flight.
These things want us to turn
from the fakery
beckoning, its shiny scansion
programmed to bewitch

   and from the ferry
   the monad peak
   keeps terror intact

      and on the plane a man
      his jokes whiplash

       *woo woo* the cloud's retreat
       *woo woo* baffled over its interior
         into the cycle

where the golden girl pivots to destruction
as if in glue, things torn slowly from her, and
here, again, as if by accident,

*curtains car torrents*
*speculation*
*nets*
     and at night an immense blue
  shuffled thru the shack like a feathered wind, and she pushed his name
   to the back of the shelf so it could not be seen, the blue things
    agitated like men in need of work. *These are the workers,* he had
     said, his name spilling across white linen.

Afterwards, description vanished, like fireworks,
following the path of disbelief, the body
invisible from its velocity.
But the workers had seen nothing, their heads
bent, shuffling among tents.

Something stuck in her hair.
Something shot full of holes.

Something igniting the minnows
                under the sea's bright blister—
                                afterlife of silver, wreckage of bronze.

Now the mouth is closed
because it cannot describe

because dawn is gouged
because they reach the same language

desire is a fold
and repetition its music

the image collapsed
periphery unsettled

as in a picture of stars
curling through space

and the slightly moist thing
cast onto the reef, a reverie

distilled from a kiss
or a shadow along the edge

of an open fan
or along the pattern of vines

extending the night
or the code *room number x*

(because the body survives
to critique its depiction)

and gives in to the other
who prefigures the call.

*to Tom Johnson*

23

# THE SAME MOON

Are we asleep? not to confuse
the water

with no water
the graduate with her desire

(peonies, their heavy tresses
falling head first)

so this must be the drenched
precipice of the near

but the young like what is said
to be said without hindrance

*this is this, that that*
girl in new sandals

the soap's prevalent scent
last cries from afar

where a tent unfolds
so that you might find

sentimental debris
as when, in a park, you

said, and then she,
the park, of course, a lot

and the map
may be lost by now.

Meanwhile, the same moon
slips over our shed.

I seem to be counting
everything at close range

diction scrawls across fanfare
and the heart's graffiti

places clarity against
o say a green hull

whose bleached image
turns

toward the artifice of eternity
logistical flicker of wave

foghorn, bell,
so close to blurry articles of faith

stone skipped across water
lily pulled from mire

oil scent and the Spanish soprano.
Meanwhile, in an alley, a casket

opens on crude hinges
and the hermit climbs out

feet in rags
the vocabulary of rags

as it arrives, newsprint
across the blind

economy's serenade
folded into the unsung

stipulating eclipse
guest of the night sky's

ritual exchange—
take this, give that away,

take, give, take, give
now cast all back.

# SPLENDOR

The dream ascends its microcosm, making *not sense*
and the atavistic goons clash
at the edge of the park, sky
sky plumed
        all prepared
for the haunted bailiwick of strangers
trailing incognito across the past.

But the light seems musical, lowered
against the ridge
into *andante*

                *shift shift shift*

News of earth: the fabulist knee-deep in mud,
fists of green, tinsel dripping by degrees,
shoe left in the meadow,
the sentence elongated and
patched onto the war zone.
It could be dark, theatre of dark,
the unsheltered sentence bloodied,
the opaque moon, the glassed-in record,
                  the will to rise.

Call it *The Person* things will go back to sleep
as if forgotten and the difficult will seem easy
                walk into the light
                    show the precarious stays
                      set off fires from above
there will be no *one* to count no *two* to include
no *three* to beg for mercy
the trail of time will be easy to follow
good old oaks, billowing lilies along the roadside
no *four* to divide

                  the valley is incrementally cold
                  *down up down down*

    mediated by the memoir's fake torture
    and the one-way war

        panic of recognition
        dangerous evident sun.

But in the slovenly small-eyed dream, surely
we are victorious,
our kisses stamped into wet clay,
our harrowing ended in song.
*Rah! Rah!*
as the struts of tomorrow fall to ground
as tears arrive from afar in new boxes.

# SNOW

1.

The real painting is larger
                    but its
signage is in order:
each word captions each image.
Acoustical gash in the circle, the spill
called *rose,* the inverted, fugitive slide.

2.

Soiled cloth sanded, curtain
folded against flame's apex
and rant, a closed tip
whose announcement is tripped over—
ungathered, then gathered as a gate.
These trusted valences
modulate into scores, too rapid
for touch, so the thing pierces its effigy.
Pivot of chimes, rampant choral addendum.

3.

Imperturbable hoax
late initial task
to find the tally
          permits signed into deeds
          give forth onto such exits
              that the tricky god admires
                  bows down
          under the trestle
              perpetual lapse
                        stolen (only the word is stolen)
                            bewitched.

4.

Fallout: rigor's finite play
its podium or crust
                    inventory attributed to mass and

*three* and *three*

                 hopscotch chalk   ice patter
        kindred trek   wet hourglass   direct rib
               tangent arc   up as close

transom invisibly placed
massive garment massively intact.

5.

    *sheaves*   breaks into subject and object
        the attic pierced
                frame as duration
                            after the fact
untenable flotation of history
(emergency route)
*this storm is what we called progress*

hushed predicate of a previous inventor      nomad/monad     seed.

6.

Indecipherable ballet and skid
(cage)
inventoried Is
tears at an egg's comatose shell

      brittle ingredients
           scatter Goliath.

7. *(Adorno to Benjamin)*

The realm where history and magic oscillate
about the duty on wine
about the barricades
about the arcades
             a mere as–if
                    the wine and the town gates
        spontaneity, palpability, density

crassly and roughly omits
calling things by their names       facts

8.

Onto this spot
comes the enchanted dupe
skirted in wares, nativity in doubt.
Only a list, only a procedure, only cunning in its way.
Out of which the beloved
paints a Tree broken into snow wings,
the unprotected pocket or crib yawns:
*I predict your unborn sorrow.* Sleep crumbs
melt on the path: *decor, the fox, the sibling dream.*

# INTERLEAVINGS (PAUL CELAN)

Snowfall, denser and denser,
a knight's breath

Snowfall, as if even now you were sleeping.

A collar of cold at his neck
above it, endless,
a foreign sky.

Below, hidden,
where my hand held the soft stuff
*was den Augen so*

prone, entire

almost fetched home into its
delay, the cast-off limb
posted.

The watch and music
in twin branches:

what body falls through the bridal mass?
Is the colored cloth a flag?

# A NOVELIST SPEAKS (DON DELILLO)

Dependency on *and*
and finally this word, this simple monosyllabic word,
more important than Paris
                          —the American language
                                    —from the American

street games, baseball, adspeak,
film, riffs,
Italian-American slang of the lost Bronx
the first fiction
                  to repeat the experience

                              no coincidence
                                    an enormous pleasure in remembering
pleasure
the unmentionable shame
the last thing

a culture of endless complaint
of pleasure whose existence we suppress

this element of pleasure
the language
                          .
                                          and fate
                          a dream release that history needs to escape

                                                    brutal confinements
                          self-preservation

against the vast and uniform death
to fashion its most
enduring work
                          to wonder in those cold war years
                              terribly sundered
                                          what it all meant

iconic fury            the atomic bomb itself
our lives

a fiction
unreal to ourselves
outside our comprehension

        lists are a form of cultural hysteria

            three great attractions
            informed

                        and jazz.

# INVOICE

## 1.

In this fettle we had or maybe it was only you—
it was you, you mere, you traffic
among the doldrums of lassitude
also your fault for noticing
in the tourism when I was carrying the enormous bunch of lilac
and wanting to buy a pad, a notebook, in DC,
something on which to write,
but the man in Hallmark said, *No, we don't carry that*
looking up from his newspaper.
Then my car was towed by the City Marshal.
Her name is Linda Swift; the stamp is her signature.
Or, rather, her signature is a stamp.
She said, *You will have to go to Brooklyn.*
Charming. Only I got it in the wrong
order: first the car towed, then the lilac, then Hallmark.

## 2.

There are two types of decision. OK? Your type is the one that comes
first, as a result of a selection from among things: words, or colors, for
example. Mine is of the second type, where the choices are piled up into
a sort of mutation, from which things are culled or pulled away. This is
how I think about it.
F is for file. Joke.

## 3.

Do you hear voices? How many? Are they singing or
just chatting in the hall?
Because everything is afloat doesn't mean there is
no track or that
no one will drown.
They promised me a domicile in which to age.
A cask.
Irony might be the price of faith, but
believe, nevertheless, in the
intimacy of the skip,

the intimate skip.
This train is making skipstops.

                         *"Beckett's art of impoverishment is in part*
*an attempt to save consciousness from the contingencies*
*and in part an attempt to save consciousness from*
*the temptations of novelistic invention inherent in mobility . . ."*

4.

Thanks for

5.

Thought, by this measure, is *"the excrement of being."*

6.

I'm sorry, I was wrong.
Here we have an example of *"the domesticating clarities of narrative orders."*
Try this: *"by a particular kind of replicative insistence, which I shall try to
define, it erodes its own statements and thereby blocks interpretation."*

7.

Choices in this suburb are scraped from the bottom of the pond.
O look, I found a boat.

# C IS FORGIVING

At the cartoon's injunction, the page limit. How now bright C
are you sated yet? Here your testimony finds an emblematic locket
to carry, like wealth, in a hip pocket.
The cup is full of questions
whose answers are tempered with clues
caustic as news from the Old World. I mention this
only because the chains are long, and the taste of salt in my mouth.
The tea service and the tiny goblets make
icy sounds underfoot
and the ground contains
cut glass. Our feet bleed.
When whispering is scented my arm,
under sleep's candor, cradles
your head lost in such dreams
as include an afterimage but
whose frames are prayers. Our claim ticket is for
nothing, although it conceals knowledge of what is lost.
I thought I could see you
hunting for something to swallow, something to tuck
under your scarf—an ear-shaped handle or the liquid
C of the moon poured from the vat of night.
Come quickly, before it empties into dawn.

# FRAYED EDGES

Domain at hitherto causation    listening booth       page

       *will show you who is right, has stood the test*

    anecdotal soul

*a la carte*
                     *lay the blame on, bear the blame*

    Too late          *na na*
new neighbors have arrived
in their slender

        *that's another pair of shoes, dead men's shoes*

     they
have descended the ladder
to the philosopher's hole, his

            *spider and butterfly and bird.*

        Here find the linear broken below
    a human form—
        hard shell of certainty,
    parody and reverence braided together,
    tiny beats of the heart—

           traced back to that other plan
      eternally existing

       *the young doing such a thing,*
  *the big, what's the big?*

    cabinet of curiosities, what
you may be looking at, unexplained.

Now I am newly sad although my house is fine:

a *silver pencil, a distinction, a thing for him.*

In the gap between sadnesses.
a man is talking and I

> *will come, it is probably a shame*
> > *and you are a pattern of tact, come to deceive us, but I*
> *I cannot the infinite*
> > *(as a child, no harm)*
> > > *but I'll try*
> > *aloud, not guessing, I would have telephoned,*
> > *thirty miles*
> > > *much, well, highly*
> *over what I have said, so*

so thought
abrades first proof. This opinion flatters
no previous *flourishing*
no surefire procedure, as when
three into six gets two.
Five into five gets one.
The catastrophic interim is here
in the cold

> *foxglove, foxglove.*

Against whose mercy shall I apply my wares?
Clarity pins us to our cause
as we walk down aisles of flameproof trees.
I am pointing at what is not there.
You are standing as close as a child.

Let us show the cat a film of crows.
Explain

> *one of the limbs or organs by which the flight of a bird, bat, insect,*
> *angel is*
> > *effected, part in, corresponding to,*
> > *supporting part,*
> > > *and comes on the wind,*
> > > > *takes under, his are sprouting,*

                                        *high, low, and the north was added on the beat*
                    *which spread,*
                            *and the arrow with eagle feathers, the shaft and ambition,*
        *his spirit,*
                            *the steps, the horse, the god*
                                        *and Victory, its way to its mate, the air*


Explain

            *blue, brown,*
                        *of day, in the wind's, right, left,*
                *beam, mote, clap,*
                        *up to the, open, wipe,*
                            *throw, cast, hook,*
                            *glass, bath, cup*
                                    *bright, brow*


Now the sky seems beautifully organized
but everything we care about is flawed.
The pool fills with leaves.
The funny pains of aging, artificial tears, and the false

                    *verdict in the note,*
                    *drawing on her pride, her shame, her position*
                                *and step at the start, before the mirror,*
            *without the medium, without coin,*
            *despite the prophet*


                    and the audience still waits for a voice from afar.

Out in the yard sparrows itch at the ground
and the grave flags flicker on their sticks.
In the coming years, you will find

                *a treasure,*
            *favor and mercy, at the feet where there is no sense in it, although the*
            *terms are reasonable. How do we*

                *ourselves? We must take it, it pays, it pays,*
            *almost impossible, but necessary*
                        *with time to read,*

                         *courage, heart,*

                                        *one's way*


to where another is, crouched
under the day in a ghost file.
How bright the fence in sunlight!
And how acute the transformation, in which


                    *a caterpillar becomes a butterfly*


and what is really there becomes a jingle about Paradise
as a red car. The red car is really there
driving along the big streets
with the soprano singing her tune
and the young man with long black hair
smiling into the wind.


The crowd
behind the barricades, trying to see
suggests something


              *a fine blossom, pierces beneath things,*
                    *and that there is a reason in it, good*
              *enough for an outward display. Why did he do it?*
                    *To give it away, to give her what is enough,*
                    *and fair, to give it all away.*


The price is merely a sweltering crypt
where drawings of saints


        *Saint Paul and Saint Michael, Saint Peter, Saint Andrew, Saint Elmo,*
              *Saint Bartholomew, Saint David*


drip pink tears, and the two-note hum
in the dead of night.


                    *na na. kap shus*
                         *rr rr*
        *loo ahs          anpay          kistre*

The churchgoers move inside, the chorus
in another room sounds victorious. Someone
drives by, blue canoe
strapped on, headed for the river.
The reverie begins again
near the silt path in front of the trailer.
People seem to need a reference
else the shore
is too far to be traversed. They want to know,
is it typical as well as indigenous,
is this an actual archival wound or repro,
spliced together by the magician

    *who would not have it, saying the living is in it, that it came to him free.*

In a sliding scale
each thing refers to another,
scandal and code
fall together in a new font.
We cross the Bridge of Triage
swaying high over the river.
Down through the murk
a cluster of shapes, black
and dandelion yellow, swift by.

Today, at the House of Anemones,
a woman called herself mad.
She confused me, in her quiet barn.
I bought a bouquet of violent flowers.
The thing refuses its gospel.
The humped range is not shiny enough
to reflect instruction's bliss,
the luminous arc dispersed without shelter.
Try climbing over yourself, try
breathing on the glass a valedictory kiss.

A dispatch of boys
made the water rise,
came forward
roped into eddies, ripping

lilies as they came.
The Beautiful Writers
in downtown Shanghai
wear silver on their toes.
They study aphoristic slang.
The empty dress floats
toward the horses
galloping out from night's tarnish.

*Na na,* theater of vigilance, graphic cloud.
*Na na* visceral digest, spitting birds.

Leave, yes, but to where?

 *Is Heaven? Did you read that? Are you going? Showed me they were, but does it touch our interests? Are you looking? Shall we, if prices fall now? I don't know, to have is the sense of it, is the use of trying. Places they sing. I am weakest in facts. Your treasure. Go. You like it, send him. He will be taken care of, the ancients knew nothing, we know little. That's it. Do you come from? Are you going? The whens are important.*

*Na na.*

*to Ann Hamilton*

# FREESIA ERRATA SLIP

"The flowers, of course, came to a standstill"
                              should read
"The flowers, eventually, came to a standstill."

"The flowers, eventually, came to a standstill"
                              should read
"The flowers, meanwhile, came to a standstill."

"The flowers, meanwhile, came to a standstill"
                              should read
"The flowers, however, came to a standstill."

"The flowers, however, came to a standstill"
                              should read
"The flowers, naturally, came to a standstill."

"The flowers, naturally, came to a standstill"
                              should read
"The flowers died."


*to Elaine Equi*

# ON A STAIR

## (1996)

*The question "where is the thing?" is inseparable from the question "where is the human?" Like the fetish, like the toy, things are not properly anywhere, because their place is found on this side of objects and beyond the human in a zone that is no longer objective or subjective, neither personal nor impersonal, neither material nor immaterial, but where we find ourselves suddenly facing these apparently simple unknowns: the human, the thing.*

—GIORGIO AGAMBEN

*Where now? Who now? When now? Unquestioning. I, say I. Unbelieving. Questions, hypotheses, call them that. Keep going, going on, call that going, call that on.*

—SAMUEL BECKETT

# INVOCATION

Speak, Mistress Quaker, a parable waits from which
blessings issue, conditionally, as in a hunt, a possible hearing
wherein the manifest flirts, beguiling, almost at home.
Speak on, Troubled Specter, as in a calm
carefree silence whose message embraces its
quick. Seed that, so
the trail is viable, literal, glad
as in love's timing: tick-tock luck.
A siege of incipient cures! A brevity so enhanced
the Pilgrim finds her way along the path of red berries
through the wild into the dilated Spot where following ends and begins
and ends again. *You were in a tale,* a choice you had not made,
whose dim constellation gathers dew on the sleeve of hours,
the iteration of just cause, saving one against the others, as in a court.
Be kind, Mistress of Woes, Hooligan of Ages. Be a Treaty we sign.
Chafe against brittle nudity, swallow the excellent potion,
remain among thieves.
Remain among thieves, steal Advent from avarice, dark from idiot sight.


*to Bernadette Mayer*


47

# ON (*Word*)

O but the sky! Unhinged *junket junket*
traverse Perpetua the jays, the trucks—
these are violent times
and our songs are old.
Hast seen a ghost? Hast fled a tree
collapsing on your head? And the snow rushes.
And the storm passes.
*Are we mere vocabularies?*
I do or do not believe in God.
She does or does not love him.
He did or did not commit a crime.
The hairy-armed man is dressed
in the flowered frock of his second-grade teacher—
A Mrs. Flood from Columbus. He carries
a large shiny handbag, a gun, a camera
to record their vacation on the east coast.
He is or is not a woman.
Words turn on the mischief of their telling.

# ON (*Thing*)

And then having to hide under the thing
the rubber cone or tent
at the foot of a virulent tree
and then she, in Paris, with her hair newly cut
leaving on a train for some place else
and I unable to decide
stranded at the deception
among strange shoes
and the dull ornaments of a regime.
The amber light of the mother is
thickly spread, and patches of carpet
shag green
planted on the sidewalk
to imitate moss, although moss is never there.
Pushing this aside to get
under the floor, below the written, as
in a black winter pond, a cistern
or pipe or throat—
circling purple fish, shadow of an arm, toy boat—
voice thread thru stone, between the *s* and the *t* and the *one*.

*to Rick Moody*

# ON (*Dream*)

Had then the dream *cash* (something persistent)
from bed to bed, unanchored
as from earth to fire to air
*crash* or *clash* or
the memory embodied in its shape
a man with a gold portfolio
behind a wall, a villa, its shape
larger than *earth* or *water*
unattached to the sign at the side of the house
unattached to the dress
not the tiny bird on the long dark bough
calling *me me me*
not plastic scissors (a cartoon)
great drift of ragweed
melody crouched under noise—
o thing, you cannot cradle this relic
as it travels thru what is.

# A CLOWN, SOME COLORS,
# A DOLL, HER STORIES, A SONG,
# A MOONLIT COVE

1.

*Ur* said Clown from a shelf said Harmony Clown
from his seat on the shelf before Is

*ur ur* said Clown, repeating the said

> from a dusty
> green bike
>
> from
> a thicket of
> keys
> a dump under
>
> clover
> from kiss

from the Tale of a Tub, an awful color
an unhealed lump

from the Dwelling of Dwellings
*ur our Urn* said Migrating Clown.

*Is this field's dementia, its prow?*
*I am thirsty in the aisle*
*in the shallow preambled space*
*below this whatnot sheet*
*above that rusty brow.*

*Am I safe or for sale?*
asked Clown from his crib.
*Do I have a use?* he inquired.
*Will I fall will fly is there*
*a bridge or a still?*
*There's a rose on my nose,* said Clown.

*The laws are erased/I cannot see from this echo*

*the locked port and grimy window/I think I saw*
*boughs with few inoculators/air was not part of*

*that scene/I am missing*
*part of my throat/my mouth jumps*

*Am I lost or stolen? Did I belong to a thing?*
*Did I live in a tent or a stream?*
*Are these eyes borrowed? (they seem to be used)*
*Did I once have a sex? Is it this?*

2.

A coin caught in a bramble like a tear in hair

       *This would be Silver*

An arrow or error/no marks
reef dismantled/pearls
roll under ebb tides

    mercurial tracks scalded

       *This would be Yellow*

I am made of newsprint and milk
my feet and hands are wax

I have no boots to hike thru Jerusalem

       *This would be Black*

I am in need of stilts
in need of transition

something to follow/a wall to dismantle/gauze for my head

       *This would be Green*

Please find me a thread near the river
a ribbon for my throat
Is this hope in my cup or a sock?

*This would be Red*

Incessantly stripped world must I enter
your chamber/I live in the morning's attic

Am I poor or wise?
Am I awake?
Am I bride or nun?
What is fun?
I know I am strange and fake

Must I go to the spot where the man is?
I'd rather not

*This would be White*

3.

The party folds, finds its coil
After such, a pattern of such.
A third is needed, coins for change.

Illegible me
crater under a sky heap.
Coins for turning from the inexact.

Dancing out there on the rim
enthusiasm among shy animals.
Remedy of the solution, however inexact.

Leaving out a day, and another day
a poison is about to be swallowed.
A solution in bright water.

Prim armature, and the belly
coming undone in exaggerated formats.
Snow to water, water to mist.

Watch.   Whatever could we watch?
An accident televised? A rebellion?
We missed the final episode, the revenge.

Not blamed because
the incident was not recorded.
Revenge over coffee, the sweet good-bye.

Farewell, holy one.
May the exit be deft and merry.
*Good-bye, good-bye.*

4.

Afternoon's misguided handle
dangles on itself and beyond.

*Laughter is the remedy,* he said
from decorum's permanent cage.

Yet the tree, the tree doesn't laugh.
What is that bending and giggling?

It's a heart in a field of hearts
trying to pry open the locked jaw of air.

A cast of thousands newly installed
in a democratic regime.

An iterating mirage,
the what for which we search.

And the new bloom in the window box?
That too is red, but is kept behind bars.

*It's a parade,* he said
from under the annals of greed.

5.

Fled, said Doll, eyeing
the shadow of a shoe.

What leaps? What falls?
Is noon cast off?

Not yet blooming as aftermath,
sequence stunned in a bud

a blush of erasures, of prints.
Someone, not me, was here

dreaming of day, as of
inclusion.

One shoe hopped away.
(If what opens fails to open

is it asleep?)
This does not fit.

Outside, is it infinite
or just dark?

6.

The solitary design is not inherited.
It says of itself *shadow, veil, shadow*

inventing a smile in the mirror
with pink lights. It has eyes

because the child sees herself
as an oval tracing

disguise after disguise, her
picture and merit.

Under a reprieve
an orchid

*innuendo*

                    upscale as flotsam on a hearth
                         breathes innuendo

                    and a collection of meanwhiles
                         ravenous for more

                                        filters thru
                              the quotidian spray

            scented by
                 pathology of an adventure
                      its lesions

            in Paradise.

                    The children are weeping
                    the dear one is afraid to come home

                    to the rage of material
                    laid out in print

                    an opening
                    not to be shut

                    by any such kisses
                    or the rags of the twisted clock.

                    Berserk in artifacts
                    he continues to pray.

And the mirror
is inside the house inside the mirror.

There is observation of the sky
from there, although the curtains are closed

as if winter.
Winter in cause after cause, each

held by a clasp, a
hook and eye, a row of small

pearl buttons with thongs,
their crescent nails

the milky sheen
of old porcelain—

hairline webbings,
leaks. That night

a single candle gave forth its meager scent
and the lovers sat staring into it

as the trough of water
rocked gently—

hypothetical desire
cast in real wax.

7.

Unremitting architecture of trust.

8.

*The Book of Hanging Gardens.*

9.

Visits to Zoos and Sanctuaries.

10.

Once I knew a Tree
in an episode of doing
it was a lesson in leaving
I did not learn.
Among my friends much is forgotten.
Once, in a crowd, there was
fool's gold, oceans of musk,
awful procedures,
cold dung.
I cruised there
in ample foraging hunger.
Black nets over beasts
enormous as mountains
swift as elevators.
Big jokes above the city.
Arcane paths or patches
and food, hot food, for scholars.
Is this a circus or a cloud? I asked,
watching the cast of lights
in the sky.
*VA*
and *vA*
and *variation* said the sequel
blowing its tune into vapors
political and dumb.
*Without attachment a riot.*
Even a Clown knows that.


11.

Silver ship
            darns under the moon, severs a little mercy.
Some gifts were left above the meadow
they are
storied in the picture
they are a tune in the sun *the ugly sun.*

Some gifts where the young are laughing, tearing themselves into
small trinkets, into
clipping knots. And up there is speech
with a smudge, the dirty hand of the night
harming its mouth. Now it will never say *yes*
never say *Hi, this is*
*my music in a box*
*this is my hand reaching into a pocket for keys.*
It wants to sit up, make it sit up!
It wants to sleep, sing it to sleep.


*Lullaby of the Moon*


The floor gathers an unseemly rate
obituary or fortress *(fate)*

spine of fields
finality or spindle *(yields)*

beautiful endurance
royal furl of the carpet *(dance)*

on each cusp a dove
on each palm a grove *(love)*

wherefore she hangs her home
from a string, from hair *(comb)*

last fling of domain
faultless cove *(rain)*

carrying a city within
fine tool of belonging *(skin)*

demeanor of the lost
side by side in the arch *(cost)*

your king, my flame
ascending to silvers *(name)*

and steady as a hand's reach
where the river is *(teach)*

inhale the dawn
it carries your every pore *(spawn)*

12.

Sleep, mute pietà

*flame of sorrow* it would say
into silent thunder

                    so the heart
under a cotton chamber
parked under gray loam

        —away swift Orion trailing his belt in the pond
                —away haggard dim sisters
             —away Andromeda sipping mountain mist

    stops

*raggedy raggedy*
bachelor with broken hair

gracious avatar
turned from the entrance

no fear of the slender doll with gold rings at her waist
thighs taut as sails

no fear of the stench of a hand
sheathed in cruelty

the puppeteer's fingers
guiding the weapon, the lance.

Turn, beloved face
to where the mask is unmade

(Joe and Jane married on Saturday
agleam with it)

and two boys
swim toward each other

such fine eyes

                    such finesse—

As in the quantum delirium of a toy god, rushing into captivity
white engine on a screen seeded with
hooped wings gesticulating, wheels rapid as vermin
in last flight, from whence the saints came one by one
to the celebrity camp to dip their eyes in clover.

Hey, Moat Man, have you no nickels, no game
to foil our figures, to
salvage our estimates? This naked thumb
has for its integer *abstain,* has
for its food *suck.* Will you close my eyes?
Will you shave my pelt? In this auditorium
we are an offering, a crust, a pitter and patter
you cannot mimic.

*The cliff is*
*Greek where I go*
*with large hands, my embrace*
*(pray that the road is long.*
*full of adventure, full of knowledge)*
*tidal in effigy / tallow ebbed from the heart / cut at the heel.*
*Biographical incision, I will see the very garden*
*you intended to plant.*
*Angel of Time, are you so absent*
*I must trade this shelter for that?*

Nest in a rock slit, unfledged creature
cast upon sand.

Witness no Voice.

# NOCTURNAL REEL

*Denouncing or affirming, their vision fed on the distance between promise and fact.*
—SACVAN BERCOVITCH, *THE AMERICAN JEREMIAD*

She saw that setting was everything she could know, but that
its cause was stupendous and wretched. Everything
required her gaze, as if that alone could repair it.
Across the evening a man on a bicycle poured by
and this seemed an emblem of time racing—the acute thing
manifest and then gone like a brute song in an unknown language
summoning
all to drill. A residual tune kept playing until
it fell into a compost of notes
mouldering in the fields, taken up here and there
by the morning's adrift gleam, as if caught
on nettle, the bright noise of birds,
dull flit of petals fallen on blue stone.

And whatever constellations thus begun, freestanding
in occupied territory—*25,000 objects*
*made by craftsmen, admission free,*
*soil peeled away like old skin*—all this
changed, exchanged into that.

                And whatsoever is begun—

on her knees, framed
above and below
the contusion in the mouth
flawed into saying

                    (a still arrow

                            falls

                under the wound

                                    (another
            partition (picture's aporia, metaphorical gash

                    gaunt precipice of the near
                              (early, earliest ground
                                             lilac ash
                                    broken urn
                         summoned from the truant by the guide
            back on track
                         (the plan to build an extension
                    lethal map
            angle of descent
staircase.


In such streaks of riot
she forgets the object
*to wander to create a vacancy to forget*
and drops a stitch.
Was there a body wrapped in a canopy? Things
happened within it, thorns migrated
at the wrist as if sealed,
closely watched, a boy's collection of soldiers
marched on the kitchen tarp.


                    I detaches
enters the disparate pool

                              The carpet
                              The cup
                              The cello
                              The gun
                              The bracelet

It was (as if
            a slight memory of wet pine, thunder
                    immobile overhead
                         she had forgotten to say
                         and so scattered
                         one by one


                              for omission, for delay
            so that weapons hung overhead
                    in a bouquet
                                        (as if bequeathed

                              (as if her hands held an infant's head
                                    dead bird in eaves

decomposing
the familial nest.
(Not) being thrown
into care, the bloods scatter

                              Garden) garden

                                   stone cast into her mouth
                                   (under the knife)

                                             layered leaves, their
green resemblances, their
difficult spots
destined to go a little way down the path.

Silence prowls
so that the mind of the listener begins to wander
under the canopy of what has been said
which is only night consuming itself,
iteration by iteration, into silt. Confession
drags biography into view like a saint briefly captured
in a photograph: blurred image of her smile, flames
cascading upwards into sample peridition—sacrificial,
sacrifice always naked, as if just minted, as a star is minted by night.
She places herself there, in music's pocket, the temporal glee
restored, tale told, the deed released
thru an opening
the way a flower, despite all watching, opens.
Is this voice—remnant hum of the living,
message replayed—sufficient? Will this syntax
keep (forbidden or preserved) promise from fact?

# A VALENTINE FOR TOMORROW

1.

Capable as this, where only moments ago
we were in a generation (captive
    (precedent soothing its path—the bad joke, the blunder—
having spent these days in an addition of fears
                 (layers, telling it this way
whereas the flair (rhetoric of a bird) had come so far to ease
         forget reference, it burdens the noise *hey we just wanted to
change the*
           old enough to know better
                    and so a future which is not the far
                     the other coast
        *singing*
                  (awake all night and the
thing wants to
        arrest)
     that was a memory of sorts so forget it

                    how can we be news?
                    win, lose

we have this couplet
the rhyme is under the nest
and under that is
private.

2.

Boxed in furthest containment, troved, methodic
in range to get there from here
play a tune to your guests they might hum along
might sing take off your clothes be nude
make your heart visible as in a painting heart-shaped
recall the hand touching the skull
the luminous mouth calling *blue*
the step of the feet on the cool tiles dancing
put on your wings fly
out of range into the storm

pluck out the splinter, bleed
the tree will reveal long grains
flowers subside
there will be a dusting of spices and the scent again of the stairwell
toss your rings to the alchemical wind
the rampant vehicle of jest
the blunt gargoyle
will limp out from the blizzard
carve its face in snow, now shall pass now
in a glittering parade
and the mobile digressive figments collide
legacy of heavens where darkly dressed figures scavenge for stars.


3.

But I know a way
where the ligature of morning is even with the stars and
before that, on occasion, off and on into Friday, whose voice is the voice
—nocturnal reverie without the captured
dove. What you say, how I adhere
so prayer comes ghostlike and erudite
into the coffin's partition, and the unanimous speech of angels—
their incomplete test. Light in the window (a quotation)
is how we notice
discrepancy—*hello, hello, I forget*—incendiary fuel
tearing roof from house, rats from dream,
acquiescent cloth draped over the little town's vocabulary:

*If I sweep all the streets will you hold the dustpan?*
*If I fly to the moon will you watch?*
*If I send you a book will you press the petals?*
*If I tell you I'm cold will you uncover my heart?*

Adrift under the forgotten speech of our halcyon days when the club
met down by the sea and graduated at dawn in pink dresses,
when the pavement was good for walking
toward a park, in spring
there was spring then pinned to the pillow of a girl
asleep on the surface, her hair scented with it, ringed
with desire. *I dare you* is what we said

to the old god drunk as a skunk at the bar
as the obligatory craft of strangers rattled the cage.
Out all night visiting the tide as it swept over the city's rapture—
ritual drum answering, turning to steam by morning.
Now we could see a normal oracle blinking and cruel
humming a tune on the boardwalk—

*If I swallow your seed will it fill me?*
*If I follow your lead will it kill me?*

and a child with a pail and some sand and some glue.

# STAIRCASE

Stay. A legible harmonic twins the harbor.
There are choral episodes
among the sails, and the kingfisher's plunge.
Stay. A petty wind fingers heat
like a girl her curls, gazing out
at the ensuing collision. A woman,
steering into floodwaters, is swept into a canyon
in Tucson, Arizona. Had she read Empedocles?
Had she recently wept? Light
infected leaves, then drab, then
heavily attired
the ephemera of air's
sway, window to window, like a disembodied
wing, its passage wholly unrecovered.
In mournful arousal
a flame cascades, as if to touch the end.
Something waits in the pristine normal blue,
a Saturday, or love, or a city besieged.
The effects were known; they were the lived thing
ardently collapsing into a distant litter:
remote pages to be burned,
the wake of a small green boat
allotted to a scrim, or Paris,
or Celan. How beautiful, how untrue!
is what historians would say
as the white frothy stuff swept over the bow
not ever acknowledged—
not yet counted, not yet
found. There is the
ferret, Luna, lost in the woodpile
in the dog days of August.
Someone called Matthew, and someone called Tom,
move across time, as across a bright lawn, while
a felicity steers into moonlessness, where
one might say *not a matter of seeing,*
*a matter of touch.* Homer, for example,
finding his way down the staircase.

*to Jonathan Schell*

# DAYLIGHT SAVINGS TIME

Unimpeachable wilderness indicted; sagacious sea
at the herald stage, the stain of arrest.
The red berries are poisonous, the land
trembling with gaslight, muddied by glass.
Could this be forward? She knocks
at the frugal door as the train stops at the strand
averting a tragedy. This would be spectacle and so
a film would come out of the dusk
so that we are stranded with morning
tucked under the wreck, and the beloved voice
not anything anyone could hear. The iconic delusion
starts to cry real tears as she picks up the corpse and goes on.

*But your voice has changed,* and here is my favorite ghost
asleep in bed, in the midst of other bodies.
The throat—as if in memory of a friend—
empties itself under the roof
of the double roof. She lay in the tinsel light
grafted there, still as a doll,
and tried to say this word, this *garçon,* is not
the blond lad striding into malty night
at another's behest. Here I appear as my father's
worst dream, in which the opening to the tent
shifts into a riot of possibilities
and his sense of belonging is turned to a nomad's rite
high over the desert on a high plain. A ring of hair
is presented for good service, but he covets the sword
passed from one to another in a ceremony
with a figure at the helm, bejewelled and calm.
The linen frock she wore on the tennis court
was a prelude, but it too
landed in the bin with rusty armpits
and buttons lost in a basket of lost buttons.

The dawn is too dark for words.
Obscurity is wanted like a ditch
out of which an embrace might be figured

the day we were lost in the woods
and waded thru muck at the edge
of an artificial lake
in the shape of a kiss, fish drawn on its sides, lilies
engraved on its surface.
I had forgotten my camera
so there is no evidence
and you have asked me not to tell.
Others are free
to imagine another story
flipped from pages of a book they intend some day to read.
It was only an imitation landscape and this is still a draft
purloined from copies awaiting notation.
Too many names were dropped along the way
lint everywhere and you are invited to
a future as the doves
dip their tails in water and make their
noise. The day keeps raising stakes
and I thought how the particular could be non-pictorial
rising and falling like a conversation
instantly erased. *Hello, hello. Good-bye.*

# BLAKE'S LAGOON

Here rendered
below the rim

going down
under the silence

where the eyes of dawn
seek the eyes of dusk

something like that
blinking

the mutable screen
lingering

        (sun, more sun, so much sun

                it must be a porch of

                          renovated time

                    the longest string held across centuries

                    an extended drop

            desperate altar

              nave shimmied into least zenith

                unpaginated, balanced

                    ) was it a curve or

              a telescopic dot saying good-bye in

the rain/I think it was a

figure musically witnessed, weather, your face, object

indigenous and unremarked.

As if

      to re-vision

providence

      redeem erroneous Providence

the delusory rainbow

a covenant that gives birth

the Shadowy Female whose garments are garments

                *milky pearl, clouds of blood*

      The place of her protection

surrounded by limbs

delusory covenant

          (blank)

who announces the message which

mirrors her journey

          the Eagle of prophecy calling

the lovers, the contraries

to view their

embrace

at the edge of the *sea of time and space* (not

a Death Couch, unbound

                       *sexual garments* into *Human Lineaments.*

I will empty this dish

Time has no name for it

it will not grow

made of glossy air

                     materials as if plangent or spread

                        where the tangles rivet sound into fan shapes

                               *Will we ever get out of here?*

The corner's triangular glass

affixed to an object

(how these visions thwart passage from bed to bed

one honored, one

                     by light) deleted.

# NIGHT BARRIER

Men assemble in a trussed league
whose least crime is not known

foot after favorite foot whose biography
is quoted

       at the gate

of the subject.
Three into three goes?

Last things first, and the itching contusion
of accident *(after chance rolled thru)*—he said

something about a monkey and lo!
it appeared on the unguarded screen

confirming

Logos

      into library and our aspiration

the black
mark on the white

present, to present
an age

shrunk to a stipend or clock.
There must be, if there must be

obsidian halo
grassy knoll

over in the contingent dream
historical marker

this not knowing is not a lacuna

grassy halo
obsidian knell

three men in blue shirts smiling
their modest affirmation
workers

in pursuit of
another possibility

haunted
by the swerve

the crisis and feast
fatal response

to dust
like an idea of dust

angelic, atomic

                    whose shadow moves from hand to mouth
                    filling its motion

with infiltration, a thing
whose imprecation swallows
the ground on which it strides, a paltry ghost's
birth.

                    Change me, it calls, into
substance, a home, garden overlooking a vista,
blossoms, a path, the sea
wherein practice is performed
as the twilight's
confession: Father, I am deliberately
missing the events
by which time is told.

I refuse nourishment, I am
an old woman
ranting on a stoop.

The girl is always dancing behind the leaves.
The fish are always swimming on the screen.

# POISE ON ROW

Look laminated dichotomy/field
sutured to field
open your mouth an ocean is within
chronic diaspora
                          open open
tribulations of a            *say aint*
                                dust star
                                    pollinates


centuries of dew.

And were we to anoint these commodious villages
the eagle would be

high over the perfect V
                                    vintage/voyage hell's mermeronic clip
                                        in the glaze of meaning's cup


its logo
itching to be born.

Prudence and Wisdom calypso thru the dark wood, overtly
semantic, while we on trial
obey the moon's hooded grief
whose October is sentenced.

The fool is enticed.
There it is, the display itself,
her nude retreat across the carpet, fictive and mean
as Hopper's vulgate.

What we see is the custodian's lament
—vile Hermes, vile trolling Spirit
raided with alarms

arms relented into an easy clasp
iterated on the path of the prey

as the mock angel, shadow's lilting encumbrance,
feathers his nest.

Just here you might find the gregarious animosity of sorrow
sworn to duality. The tongue
is forked, lathered with desire
and printed thus, and the spin or pin
hits the old heel

           there is a hand held
                the thumb anchors
                  in a torn book
                    and this thumping god
                        stammers across the threshold

   *blu*

     *pur*

*gre*

*um wu*

    *songdirt*

      *in mir*

        *in or*

          *mar*

            *to market to market*

            sayeth the rag.

Paradise is stranged
and the net quenches.

# SEQUENCE WITH DREAM OBJECTS
# IN REAL TIME

Meandering lit space/chained
mystique of the opulent, now narrow, now culled
as keel or knoll, the uneven crest
over such river decisions
pointing to a narrative chain—second instance of the emblem
wholly uncontained in reverence
of what, now culled, now
recalled, the subject
as particular as eddying knowledge
without its little musical notes/spark of the delicate hand
reduced to

wind's terms
frightened abundance
o that house, that incident
some significant equation (
had we heard? one: the death, two: the repeated
phantasm's

meandering lit space/chained

as keel or knoll, the uneven crest
over such rivers

uncontained reverence

recalled, the subject
as particular as eddying knowledge

reduced

to frightened abundance
o that house, that incident
some significant equation (
had we heard?

now narrow, now culled

pointing to a narrative chain—second instance of the emblem
in reverence
now
recalled, the subject

without its delicate hand
o that house, that incident
some significant equation (
had we heard? one: the

meandering lit chain
the mystique
as the keel's uneven
river decisions
pointing to a narrative chain—second instance of the emblem
wholly in reverence
of what, now
called the subject,
as particular as eddying knowledge
with musical notes/spark of the delicate hand
reduced to

wind's
frightened abundance
o that house, that incident
some significant equation (
had we heard? one: the death, two: the repeated
phantasm's
frail body flared
down slope, head over
heels, a paper acrobat cartwheeling
down wind, making the skittery sound of things
in wind. And then
in obeisance
turned into an avenue, its
skin peeled into sight's
lesson, the trust that retrieval—
some hand, some eye—will fetch it back
to meaning's chance

night crowded into a
black bag left
near the third rail, giving my sister the pearls,
staring at the map framed in polished burl and now
the wide smiling face
smiling into some width or necessity's
this is the   they have
(chained the soldiers) chained (to the door) the door.

# FREE FALL

More comes along to sustain *flap flap* a departure
this much is uncertain in the wreckage of Verdi

or why asks the girl to her self (looks at now)
voice of the tenor currents of opus

the hand–held child mentioned in passing
day on its side too many pages

turning *if then* flat as a five
numerical exposure every thing countless

plus evocations plus seedlings plus fish
among ingredients where a kiss leaves its mark

translating habitude to the rash on the throat
incidental flight no less than free fall

Source of the whose of why of when
what map travels what speed what incentive

incidental expression then a career
o dally awhile off the expedient trail

gather a myth from the unused archive
save a place at the stop (wave to the camera)

bring some white twice as big as an orchid
the spoils of a wish the path of a snag

arrange to meet at the edge of a lip
did you smile in your sleep did you order this

beast or trigger (hand under belt)
what did he say at the close of night

among the epithets permanent (sequestered)
(could not be found) bracket our sequel

sock lost on the rug target of ruin
city of haloes of exits of sorts

*flap flap* the dragon I thought it was Sunday
at least it was under the ambush of evening

fetch me a braid the stairs are they open?
speak not to strangers they covet your tongue.

# AND THE QUESTION OF

(Note: most of the language taken from *Of Spirit: Heidegger and the Question*
by Jacques Derrida, translated by Geoffrey Bennington and Rachel Bowley)


1.

What of this meantime?

In the name of
avoidance he forgot to avoid
entangled

                         for example
the economy in those places

                            to approach, to make it appear

under a crossing out
             *pneuma, spiritus, Geist*
                 (crouching enigma, cadaverous light)

under the title, under test
the *chora* in it.
                    What is the knot, the single simple knot

at stake is the
collecting and gathering

*why*

                (method of embryonic toil, the daunting proposal
                    of resilient cups, loped dashes,
                         shattered and additive, the
                              radiant stains prior to us)
Is it already the question?

               The call, the guarding

Is it still the question?

be patient here

*pragma, praxis, pragmata*

on the hand
in the domain of the hand

between speech and the hand
handwriting
the interpretation of the hand
of hand and animal

sheltered in obscurity manifest

*the stone is without world*
*the animal is poor in world*

now withdrawn   the examples of the chora
the ambiguous clarity
these four threads.

2.

A leap, a rupture
out of the question, out of the way

and, in silence,
(a thing, reality, thing–ness)
the I and reason
goes without saying
Now who are we?
We were speaking a moment ago of the question.
You cannot say that a stone is indifferent to its being without
*I am, you are.*
Not at all that of the stone or the tablet.
The stone is placed
before the difference, between indifference   *zu fragen*
the root of the who
the absolute indifference of the stone.
We will come back to this.

3.

On the horizon

a task, destiny or a further becoming.

I don't see, I do not know which—*spirit, soul, heart*—

yes and no.

Later (along

this path

a man and a woman

meet) we cannot go.

# POEM WITH LAST LINE
# FROM EPICTETUS

Gray against further gray
her figure an allowance

walking along her own
counting or making sure

supplemental to what he might see
or to what he does see

looking out (below her)
gray against further, contiguous

sentence of plumes
the branches felled, the sway

specific pockets
where lovers spoon

woman with portrait of her son
and the other, the American,

in a war zone, upheaval of names
telling, unable to tell

so it is said *whosoever*
in an archive yet to come

evidence of what will be laid down
pasture, stone, the coastal hum

parade of dancers on Main Street
the adored who says *I am*

sky's ripening air
daily opulent rigor

bits of a body in time
*my bit of a body, you mean.*

# AND FOR EXAMPLE

## *(1994)*

*We ought to say a feeling of* and, *a feeling of* if, *a feeling of* but, *and a feeling of* by, *quite as readily as we say a feeling of* blue *or a feeling of* cold.

—WILLIAM JAMES

*Unto the Whole—how add?*

—EMILY DICKINSON

# THE PRIOR

1.

Edge of a lot vacant, wishing for that.
Covetous of what the afternoon would bring.

An errand the mind might run.

Something to do after the holiday; a spree.

After the holiday and all, still hungry.
Something worthy of news: that not tame.

In the film it was evident
there was nothing to tell. You could tell
that. Only spillage, only excess
as a form of boredom. Her breasts
and legs all decked out; lips
formatted *kiss*. His
mouth aroused by vacancy.
Streets tricked out in garbage but
no particular scent in blue air.

Something to do after the ride back on Friday.

You could tell you were moving away
from what you owned. No one knew
what to call the next one, only
that it would come and it would be the same.
Same and silent, an anonymous likeness.
Wanting to say this is not the same
*this* is not the same as *this*.

Walking across the bridge,
a fictive suspense.

Things are delivered, too many
to keep safely, to follow as the hymnal

word for word. Tune sullied by disuse;
chimes bricked up. The assumed
enclosure in need of repair.

2.

Striking out into the calamity
quest without caption

here take this highly influential ingot
this jacket, book, odd velvet

props left out over there
kept off-screen at any distance

hung from a single chain
sad stamina of the scene

a common thing
not a list, not an emblem, not required

financed by a steady gaze
the boy's bright gaze in the bright air

his mate might come with her cats
(unreliable cats on the church roof)

A slack wind and a catastrophic sail
*Ditto* said the boy, the Dante, learning.

3.

If this were speech, a speech
could it elicit the X mentioned above
of which this might be the result?
They were only playing.
Mask without face, no real tears
under the obligatory smile. Real anything.
Examples could be footsteps following the real.
He drew a thread on a wall, not architecture,
so when we looked back only bending, shifting.

Bending, shifting, usual noise, kids
yelling in twilight, tired from the sun.
They are waiting to be told to come in. *I said now.*
I said now they are waiting to be told to come in.

What is it based on what pleasure
what lost in what of your own making—

enclosure needs repair.
Boat without sail. Many tourists.

# RANCOR OF THE EMPIRICAL

A lavish pilgrim, her robes unbound,
checks into a nearby hotel.
Let us spread the wealth.
Let us speak in such a way
we are understood, as a shadow
is understood to assuage these prisms
and these mercurial clasps. She was told
*yes* and she was told *no*
which is how she became excessive, spilling
over the sequestered path, her wild garments
lacerating stones.
She took pills against rain.
She slept under tinfoil.
In that country, there were no heroes
to invent a way to fill the hours
with parables of longing, so her dreams
were blank. Sometimes she imagined
voices which led to her uneven gait
and to her partial song. Once she was seen
running. A child said he saw her fly
low over the back meadow and into the pines, her
feet *raving in wind.* The child
was punished for lying, made to eat ashes
in front of the congregation. The priest said,
*You have made a petty story. Now enter duration.*

# THE UNTELLING

The task subsides, gloating in perpetuity. This
without watching, a form of purpose
exhaled, possibly spoken.

Because of the length of knowing
valued in the first place, its name
unattached from the rigors of display,
withheld as *later,* as *before* or *after.*

Then you say
*tell me and tell again*
and I say

*The leaves are a wall.*

And she came down the stairs
intentionally.

And then the man the end.

So that later it seemed a season had landed.
And you ask *which which*
and what is it about?

Down the stairs where the irretrievables
were kept. Or: her purple shoes
are in the dollhouse. Or:

it came as if pulled slowly
as a mouth filled with awe
moves its silence slowly in a ring.
Only a picture could picture it.

And you ask
was it a kiss that did not happen on any street
to her so it did not predict, make amends,
was not an extra key, a visit?

I repeat *the leaves are a wall.*

*Explain* you say.

I say jewels sprawl before the Rat Man.
I say Cassandra at her dusty ball
her old mouth saying *what what*
*put your house in order*
*the people are turning away*
*I see fire in heaps*
*I see air perpetually stale*
*I see a stiff patch shifting.*

*Explain* you say.

I say someone I do not know told me
my Godfather Tom
was found
on 57th Street
in a dumpster.    Tom
she said looked like Walt Whitman
with a beard and long filthy nails.
He was the theatre editor of LIFE
during its heyday. He
took me to see *Waiting for Godot.* He
gave me a book on Etruscan art
a dragon from Nepal
a round-trip ticket to Paris. He said
*you are an eagle behaving like a beetle.*

You say
*the wall is on the ground*
*thank you good-bye.*

in memory: Tom Prideaux

# ECLIPSE WITH OBJECT

There is a spectacle and something is added to history.
It has as its object an indiscretion: old age, a
gun, the prevention of sleep.

I am placed in its stead
and the requisite shadow is yours.
It casts across me, a violent coat.

It seems I fit into its sleeve.
So the body wanders.
Sometime it goes where light does not reach.

You recall how they moved in the moon dust? *Hop, hop.*
What they said to us from that distance was stupid.
They did not say *I love you* for example.

The spectacle has been placed in my room.
Can you hear its episode trailing,
pretending to be a thing with variegated wings?

Do you know the name of this thing?
It is a rubbing from an image.
The subject of the image is that which trespasses.

You are invited to watch. The body
in complete dark casting nothing back.
The thing turns and flicks and opens.

# from "For Example"

*These are examples of leaving out.*

—JOHN ASHBERY

## STEPPING OUT

*It has been easy to say in recent times that everything tends to become real,
or rather, that everything moves in the direction of reality, that is to say,
in the direction of fact.*

—WALLACE STEVENS

If everything tends to become real
then whose trial has ended
on a scale of one to ten
in which three is a dream
on a floor
no one can see.
                *Also, perhaps, maybe*
elicit the shard from its fervor
to display amnesia: one person in jail
another walking across a roof
where what is written on the sky
brings formality to the event, as when
we first ask, *What is it?* The world,
loosed like a hem, is
what we step out on
and are pulled along away from our doors
not so much appeased as grafted
onto the long dark pause.
Pointing, not seeing anything, not knowing
the name for what isn't there.

But the prestige of a moment is not its name.
After all, we sleep among secrets
and wake to their burden.
If we could pay attention at all points then
theory would be what really is there. But then
another intimacy begins
while a chorus of male voices
carries the bar away/raft
of flowers brought into a girl/her body
emerging from the story as a new link
on an old sheet/ignorant single ambition of one hero
listening to another but not listening to this spring's snow.
Only the women speak of war, for example.
*"To be prolonged in the first place*
*so we dream of escape,"* she said
in the midst of history.
                              The dictionary
is part of the clutter
*lure, decoy, bait, snare, trap*
and so to cross the heart
might make us *only here* or *here only*
depending on the translation.
Was one aflame? Is this a lake?
And why is part of the flower
mentioned at night
when she finds these love knots
in another dream she cannot recall. And
around the sinuous thread the doctor
with his pen
draws a line across her abdomen like the general
in the green room with his green map and stick, his
war game of war under the strong light of the canonical:
Kafka, Freud, and whatever girls might make an example.
Festering green bar, nothing on the menu available.
*Et peut-etre* yes! now she understands why
she would rather not mention names
but what was it said of the singular? The wall
could be a *lining* or an *inner partition*
if everything tends to become real.

It's true, I was sad all day
for no good reason like a forgotten task
attached to too many site-specific verbs—
*to want, desire, wish, require, please, try, attempt*—
you get the idea. Only the finality of rhythm
on which to insist: rhythm as the example.
Now the resourceful writer becomes a drunk
as she stands against a church wall
under clear light.
Nothing is early enough, for example.
We are not located in the world but in its
particulars: what's done is done, the show is down.
Tyranny comes naturally to the dead. Was that
the perilous night
mentioned by the composer and copied
onto a page? The fat belly revealed, the wound
similar but not the same. Indifference
spoils what is real, for example.

So we find ourselves in the excess
of what is already here
and want to speed up to the good parts.
Some noises are glamorous, like dance, the
discipline of celebrated silence
but love moans and collapses
under a saturated roof
and we admit to being ruined, at least once.
The glassy eye is anointed by its tear.
If you save everything that has hurt you, you
might come close to saying its prayer
passing the basket from hand to hand
not having to memorize the empty gaze

where you just were. Then
survival could be negative space
where what might be reconstructed
has fallen away beyond erasure
to the small case before travel.
*Get back in your room.*
Is anything in childhood mutual? The lifted

parameters of touch mingle with the stung,
as when reaching up above clover
to the magics of another season
which might be serene. They danced
under an awful light, and her shoes, her gowns,
twisted in shadow; only the shadow has lasted.
The clasp of his hands on her back, for example.
The limbs of the corridor could not speak
but were folded under
where wet hair was out of sequence
on the black floor. The train
pulled its litany across a populous tread, torn
into geography and a wish to stay up later
than time, when whatever *wisteria* was would
bloom and hand down its scented ladder.
On that side of the street the boys were
always ready, but the stairs were dangerous and locked.
*To protect what is new, to laugh without ambush or cartoon;*
*to sleep safely.* It is a matter of listening, and so
learn how to depart. What is dragged behind is a
sound that is not understood, as the city
gathers and gathers, near
as what will not come back.

From up here in the bleachers
things seem real, but provisional, like a day
in which only paper airplanes sail by
eventually to cover the field.
Unfolded and flattened, they reveal
notes and pictures in colored pencil: hearts,
trees, flowers, rhyming couplets, and other
impediments of the age. And perhaps the game is
halted on account of this weather, which is only
the missing voice and truant litter of desire.
The athletes' faces hiss with sweat and rage
and Mom is picking up socks
and spare change, paying bills, lifting
the nearly empty carton of milk
off the shelf in the fridge. Her task
is to remember whatever comes next.

To her, Time seems like an all too gregarious
protagonist, not so much eager to please as
insistent and daft, adept at charming the room
full of anxious initiates into voting his way
without knowing the facts, for example.
She thinks how rain on the roof
does sound like applause as she closes the windows.
By now the airplanes are mush
and the fans have departed in their vivid multi-colored slickers
and hats. It seems strange to think
each knows where to go, although some may not get there.
Whereas all stories seemed false now
all seemed true; the confusion
was arbitrary. This spot, this
dime. She turns on the shadow of a breath
like a bird on a branch. *Touch me not*
was how it sounded from across the field, a page
torn from a journal in which she confessed
she could not wait, writing into the wait.

Maybe all absences should be excused.
The banquet, in any case, was dull;
the soufflé never rose. But things
fall on a regular basis, especially in spring,
and sometimes we hear them, petal by petal,
as when we put our ear to the chest
where the letters are kept.
Be sure to put the broken glass
in a brown paper bag so it won't cut
someone's hand; there's enough blood
in the carpet and in the sand. Even
the mattress is stained and, like sand,
indented with the shadow of weight.
This represents a decade of dreams
which also should be put in a sack or box
and shipped to a new address: strange,
how the body takes its dreams with it
like a city buried under the rubble of ages
never to be found. Strange, too,
how what is and what is not

make a quixotic braid
which, like weather, has no end
other than those we invent
to measure change. Rain again today.
You can hear it too, sloshing through the gutter
like a rope of sound. Instead of falling
you could walk downstairs
onto the familiar street, but be careful
and take your umbrella: remember, the street
won't miss you. It goes one way.

# TANGLED RELIQUARY

Tangled reliquary under all surfaces.
Nothing moon-like occurs there
only partial coves
and entrances.
How cool it must have been
in the vat of the previous
before these habits ordained the real.
Some of us must have seen each other
naked in opulent dawn, our nerves
drawn up as from an ancient well
mossy, slick, unstuck at every seam
so we enter the sleeve of history
out of which the magician pulls
his lawn ornaments: Dancer, Prancer,
Our Lady of Provocation, flags, targets,
the bluebird's house.
                            On the adjacent field
a swarm of butterflies alights
in a bald tree. This is the Tree of Change
mentioned in the lost book of A.
Her auspice was a riddle, sphinx or no
sphinx, whose meanings we can piece together
from her journals that were torn into bandages
to wrap the wounds of the dying.
Such wanton songs paginate
empirical trust and the ruse of the first place.
        Not that story again, the one we cannot tell
to the sun as it dispenses its sheen
out over the harbor, but only
how can you perform your agile sway
without shelter and without us?
So the riddle of the disembodied name
sets in motion a primal mischief
sanctioned and forbidden by the vastly gone.

This would be a good day to go sailing
or to wash the car, but I have

neither boat nor car. There's a plotless
web in the air like a banner pulling us along
into something to look back on. What
if I wandered so far
only to come here
to the relentless
you have kept in store for me
before the song, above the river,
all the names etched in stone
only slowly annealed to the
spawning wind, in whose face
we will soon be included, having been shown
the near field's shambles
and grace. *Come here*
like a shoulder or a girl's skipping step
toward evening on a Friday—lapis amulet,
Samurai sword, Chinese silk stained with azalea,
a single earring the color of a toy globe—all
stolen from a thing called April
still wet with fresh rending. *Come*
*here* in a language
once learned, only a few phrases still known:
*bonjour, je t'aime, il fait beau.*

Perhaps one of those popular, musical Sundays
would save us, galloping at high speed in, out,
only a glimpse from up high
at the revised setting crowded with tyranny.
So I wanted *once again* as a plaything, some jewel, box, horse
on which to come fleet of vision, glad to pretend.
The cartoons sailed against the brocade and the stairs
were where the prayers were kept
like instruments of torture, basking
in shade, scent of new snow, locks of hair
under glass.                   The day, however,
has spun upwards so it seems to be a sort of chapel
of divided light, and the season, punctured,
leaks down on us as from a faint dead planet.
And I had promised never again to try to put

anything back together, to obey
the errant barge of upheavals, not to seek
cause and effect in the prevailing wind. But now
shards of promise glint through a network of uneven shifts
like the wandering voice of an ancestor
on the far side of the dunes. Bricks or dunes.
But what will we tell the children? As in a photo of
two persons dancing, there are some things
we never hear. *Shout coo shout coo*
each of us not there. So one who is the one
sheathes me in his ear. Him sings his tunes
in aberrant remonstrance and I
agree to this fear he tells whose words
are what he cares to do. Both hands are up
not so much surrendered as bequeathed
to our common night. *Dear dream,*
*will you assist us, give pause*
*to any and all of these lessons, take us, each,*
*into such fond technologies that the thigh's*
*spasmodic hum frees action as well as solace?*
But the eye is dialectical and unreasoned, its gown
disembodied because unsaid. The blue floor
calls itself June and wants to lay me down
on its shine of now
and peel off the shadows one by one
until I am it. Then sail into the air
sheet after sheet, this, that, here, there,
now, then, only as real as what follows.
That the balloon man lost his head
that the screen fell to the floor
in a heap of landscape

                    *such mornings*

that the clay pot
lay in shards/that the dry flowers were cast
across the rug—ancient seeds, crumbs—

                              *such mornings*

and the light reached all the way into the dark
as if handing it forward from some child's grave/from the
coiled boundaries/from whatever captivity we wish to sew into artifact
but which, like the light just named, eludes us, frail and pinioned
in the glossy tablets of alchemical reserve/that the elegy is
betrayed as the child follows her hand into its sanctuary and
touches the core and unriddles the riddle in the beckoning need
that the cluster of disavowal gives way
and could not be shy—

*such mornings—*

*to Peter Gizzi*

# LOST SECTION

This *three* has been lost, twice. In the *mundane shell,* or some
wheel riding the *harrow.*

In the books there is not an adequate collection,
and her letters all ask for money, from some
*corner of the Atlantic.*

             She was told to make it up as she went along
as if it were part of nature.
That was before
the *infernal scroll*
*closed over the tender moon* (the moon
of the first and second version, both
now lost in terrains of clover and bleach
in the *mills, ovens, cauldrons*
of error).

The quotidian is not surrounded by heavenly invention:
*an aged woman* raves *along the streets.*
The key, kept at the far end of the porch, is hung
on a metal cask beyond the white plastic patio furniture
now covered with snow. It's a bright spring day
at the end of another year in which too much
was exposed, like fat flesh under a diva's robes.
Plot, according to Aristotle, is the soul of tragedy
but he fails to tell
what to do
after the end of the story.

None of this was in the first version.
I have forgotten the second.

What spills over into the blank? What form?
*The text is rich where it shares this darkness.*
*This does not relate to an invisible wind.*

Kept in the trunks of distant trees
it is not released by any key
poked into emptiness,
just as a song will not come forth from any mouth.

Understand: *I am in pursuit of the missing part.*
What I remember: foil, a loom,
a cot, cruelty,
wrappings, unwrappings,
gold embers, a robe—

     *so the robe*

*opens on an orb*
*and the case is how we find our way*
*out of the privileged cast of night*


     —I think
that's how it went. Then,

*Put your ear to her mouth and ask her to sing.*


       *Tiny slip of moon*
*seen through the cage hurts*
*my eyes. How to teach what is arrested? Those*
*hill towns beckon from their height and the wall,*
*the high wall, calls from across an alley.*
*Hark! little door, little exit*
*let me gather these boughs before they lose their scent.*

Hunters move toward their prey all the way over to the other side
where the flame gives out.

       It cold here.

Floating downstream/olive eyes
mounted above the amazed mouth of a monk/prophetic scar
angled toward earth
at the site of instruction

we are, after all
the one that speaks

as from behind the wall
quotation marks, agile as lashes, blind as bats
come to tell of the wreath. Truth? No, the wreath

$$\text{—season now scrap now}$$
$$\text{glossed as such}$$

its site
a doorknob and the hand that finds it
as when leaving is knowing when to leave
(train curving across the bridge back into the city)
and the sublime, with no example,
catapults into the silken net, O
river of scripts
presuming the endeavor is real.

Birds chipping away at dawn.
In the quarantine morning, a gentle pitter-patter of lapses.
If only we could become wise, if only we could
sleep with Athena.

                        And the magical boy, cool-fingered as a witch
stands on a glass palette, a nebula
of related shapes, not random, belonging to
something, to the same special case,
special *and* same
but hid from us as a new model forms from the old putrid stuff—

disease, commentary, foliage,
gargoyle, cup,
argument, reversal,
stipend, recognition, fate.

Yet there was a time when there were only
ripples coming in from a distant event so that,
standing at the window, something
baffles him. Is destination a tunnel, far
from ordinary experience? Something worries him,
some relic

standing at the window
watching space bend in the wind's fabric
breaching the wave's hump

the figure turning now
back into the doorway's prescience—
And yet, there was a time when time was ripples
coming in from a distant event so that
standing in front of a window, something
worries him, some relic

standing at the window
watching space bend in the wind's fabric—

*They were hoping to find bumps in this; it was a hope. If you blow up the second
resonance, it decays into more particles. When people do collisions and find parti-
cles, what does it look like? Final decay.*

—breaching the wave's hump.

The figure
turning back into the doorway as through
the lashing force, through, across, into
placing us in his esteem
ruptured, alert,
in the darkness of the dark's dark.
What comes next, *four, five, six,*
is what has not yet been counted, turning,
answering the door, letting it in.

*It cold here.*

The curtains move.

Some wind.

# SONG OF THE ALREADY SUNG

1.

The situation is not going to change.
Which situation?

Anecdote of the moon.
Held there, cast in a blitz of lopsided gas.

Or, say, a row of trashcans.
Something set to music, then lost.

Four wasps on a sill; a stench.
The last thing said. Say that.

Smoke inert; leaves
frozen at June.

To do with a lock
with the other side of a bridge with

another familiar strand of hair.
The body's epilogue: *not you.*

The confession stone turned
before the applause.

2.

It reminds me of amber.
Funny how you move them from something, the bones.

The bugs that you find in amber.
They don't look like real bones.

The something of time past—of someone working
as if they were all broken, like the mugs—

has gone awry like Icarus in his machine.
But you want to hold on, a fondness

tentative, not followed through—
different theatrical situations

whose absurdity doesn't lead the mind
anywhere right now. More complex

replicas. Diagrams. Maybe fossils.
The amber piece, the photograph

that won't change. Speak
of another kind of time

pressing flowers in a book to
remind you of what you don't have—

controlling the bones. Each has such
I mean an example is a sound.

The tip of it; a
very extended kite.

The challenge of the thing.
An average pen, for example.

Its relationship to these
pieces of light: the smallest piece.

Is it a model?
It doesn't touch bottom.

A distinct velocity, a
quivering line when

absence of color becomes color's
harmonic particularity in air.

A lot about America:
real people, real objects

fashions in color, partial statements;
a meandering, vagrant line.

3.

In the midst of a phantom inch
wild and beautiful simultaneous competing tunes
an immense scattering
to picture dissonance
among the rushes
this excerpt
say an image, face down,
never to be lifted
touched for the sake of it
the shine
and those who are not clumsy
the advantage of that
yes scooping water from a pond
child with broken net
standing at the threshold maybe

as someone's father
elicits recurrent gaps
*net of the fallen through*
attached to that
singing that tune
between desire and the actual
a theory of response
the spectator's knowledge
now's edge
inscribed, instructed to sing

that lullaby again
tell a story
put the sock on the doll
pull the dress up over her head
immersed in yellow
iconicity of a scream

4.

*The situation*
*is not going to change.* Refrain
etched above the song.
Erudition of a rat.
Mind of a turbine engine.
Luck of the draw.
Examples of what?

           To watch as the reference
floats away. Away
as nightmare or game.
Glancing across the table at another's—
the confusion distance is.
A beseeching gap as in a harbor
or panels left uncertain, occupied by
weather. What cannot be
transformed into something else.

Another in another room.
It's a bright day in a small Egyptian town
but the birds here are nervous.
I can hear her voice
but I don't know what she is saying.
A time and place for circular action: this
ends in some kind of secret
some kind of occasion
an abandoned pier
the far end of a pier
alone at the far end of a pier
some kind of bargain is drawn up
an occasion for meeting
*face to face.*

          Downstairs, downstairs
a person decides.
Talking to myself (himself) this
basement in retrospect is mine.
I am always installed on a still point
a potentially dangerous spot
a seed bed

I can build sexual fantasies

                                maybe

I can say good-bye.


A clean white space but no space is neutral.
Thumbprints. Something to
acknowledge, bring back, shadow
thrown out, cast, dragged across the gravel
repeatedly. Wanting all said all done
to save one or two—
an urge to get up, go.
No particular creed, the girl now walking
across the grass, some pages in her left hand,
I can't say what in her right.
No space is neutral. There's a man
a kind of cult figure, or hero.
Sound is a replacement for him (me).
*A house is what everyone knows by heart.*


Then the real is a very convincing show? Of course
the beam looks real, but is more melancholy
an inhalation of breath moving across
to a charged little image.
It's like looking at a forest
through the eye of a needle.
In a shop I found a dirty white vase. I
washed it; now it is clean.
There's a form of dreaming in another form
and there is the sacredness of common objects.

# OF THE FIRE

These many mouths leave us vagrant, unsuited.
Bring in some jazz, or a sleuth
amiably fixated
on postage.   There's a welter here
and accidents have happened
among revisionist families not yet indicted
by the variegated stalks of what will be known as
this year. Sooner or later all affinities
will be yielded to the public sphere, our
search ended. The light revoked,
jumping from the dish—newt, preacher, trip—
none of us can measure in the trick webbing
called talk. Not enough spit
to ease the muttering ensemble or train
back on track as the mouth is carved
into its rind.

              But then the reprehensible world
begins its testimony, verifying the impersonal
like a slate on which nothing has been written.
Glue untested in the sieve, and here
the tick of a stranger's bookcase
after the fire (referring back to it)

                              its field's

chamber of elisions/sky
wearing a tarp or dark lens
aimed at noon over noon waters, ephemeral purpose
unchained from the harbor's expectations
as the Architect of Destruction builds a cavern
hectic with tarnish. That night you could see
geometries of skeletal reason—doorways, plinths—
left in the set of the empty set
(soldiers excused now from representation
because we had not seen that war) idle furnace
over there away from us
in the exclusionary rights of what we wage
in the gravity of what we know
or do not, duration mothering her child who sleeps

in bed under the sovereign roof in the moon's lamé light.
Fire, feeding on night, moving through

        and swans!

        the ardor of it, a design
        ignited well past the sun

        now cosseted in passing
        particular bit
        of something else

        in front of the pattern
        being quick on the stair, many sing

        impeccable Florence desired as a
        woodshop and the small

        weeps back, we its matrix
        in eight sections, like journalism

there was
a blue hospital, red sweater, steel towers, malice

To ask
     *by my/until her/in a dream/to the hold*
*of consciousness/at a sunlit/in the unsaid*
*in a flicker/for/by her*
*of a deaf/of snow.*
*To the pink/in reverence*
*in her bed/before Easter/with Moses/on the edge*
*until we/of his wood box/at winter's/to her*
*on the noon/from the sky.*

              Together we have come
to this side of the bridge
and stared past it, the boys
walking on ahead their long shadows mingled
thruway to thruway and past all the glass
ejected into the glimpse: call it that, that or them.

Animation trapped on the surface, like print.
But then the Gentleman with Country Hair
appears in Miami, obscurely thematic.
He admonishes us for staring at our service
and picks up his shoes invisibly pitched—
black, black on black—all this in the river below.
Objects come round to their slogans
too arbitrary or too ornate and he calls the cat
Salem after a cigarette. (Everything not seen is
parenthetical. Night is always parenthetical, for example.)
Whatever became of the ashes? Down on the rug
the origin is printed in small print
and the first sound in the garden is there also
humming and rhythmical, its transparent plume
rising.

      To gain a mercantile blue in a catalogue of blues, its
habitual, standard, issue
already squandered on expedience: nothing to be
launched. But what do I know?
I am merely a tourist here
in the Year of the Broken Hat, have not learned
how to bow like wheat in wind, do not know
which lucidity keeps the key
while inviting another in, making a sequence.
The thing—call it *horse* or *gorse* or *force*—
appears as nomenclature only, and there's a fine
upstanding pier lengthening our stay
sorting the mathematics out to keep it afloat
under plastic hail on plastic slats.
I cannot look at myself through the eyes of others
so cannot speak for them. If someone were to ask, I'd say

                                          blue-gray November light
           lapping at sand, pale
           pinkish rocks, grass
           molting to rust, leaves
           paper weight, stillness
           facing advent
           small boat eroding a path, swans

A train
parts one space from another, and a figure, a man
or woman, there's an embrace, awkward, arms
in too many places, encumbered, helping with stuff
saying *how was your trip you look great glad you came.*
The world still more beautiful than thought, heron
low over water to show us what silence really is.

Ear to ground tells of the future, leaf on roof
reflects an opposing window's glare
as the immoderate convert comes to rest in sloth shade.
But are these surfaces to be trusted
in the hooligan now—cull, impede, dissolve—
when so many strange darlings
are ready to subvert all margins of error?
Is this a body speaking, or just
an oceanic drone come to be tamed?
To inhale such episodic smoke you must
transgress its maker, filtered up into clustered heaven
where gold trim circles the amorous unimpeded there.
Until

> *of radiant competition/on the lower/for my peaceable*
> *on my shirt/on the grove*
> *in nature's wood/in stately despair/by white of ark*
> *in today's/for consumption/on the dark night*
> *in the dark*
>         *for being themselves/in despondency*
> *on my space/out of my mouth/in the thing*
> *in the salt/to wisdom/of the dragonflies*
> *off instantly/of the surroundings/of the bearded tongue/in us*
> *of paradise/in profusion/about Heraclitus/in the crowd*
> *on nutshells/of mud/on the edge/before any excess/without limit*

Humming a tune, the heiress flees
in a flare of publicity, her amulet
or headdress tilted awkwardly,
straps twisted, green shoe torn at the heel.
Free at last, she arrives breathless
to see what the artist has done to the pool.
Many sons earlier, she had let herself

down into one of her own devising, putting
wonder to the test. Trial unto me these
watery chains, bleach my hair, condone
this lattice-work of twigs. I shall stay
in the gesture for as long as it takes
even as the fire encroaches on the very blue
we decided not to buy. The umbrella
cannot shield us from the flames.
Do not give away what you intended to keep;
do not keep what you intended to give freely
or you might find yourself impaled on the wind
footloose as a saint, your address-book
scattered into soot-filled air.
Lake project, pool improvement, water system
all are things of the past
                        through which the Greek sailor
traversed to become a coin.
Above, on that other cloud,
children run through their amazed magics
inventing as they go, their skills unforeseen.
Even the wisest of us cannot read
but for next year's introduction
in the ballet chamber's endowment: chicken
encrusted with nuts, ballerinas wire-thin.
O but the minister hath committed adultery!
O but the senator is twitching on the dais!
Luckily, we have the means
to recover from this surge of unnatural weather:
fire, flood, fire, wind
pitching houses to abstraction, hell
enacted on the screen. A pantomime of ribbons
unfurls from a non-existent spool.
When the clouds broke, you could see
the litigating flames had sentenced the hills
to anonymity. Gather your deeds
and your next of kin, they had advised, even
as a cold child came into the world with a purpose.

*to Michael Palmer*

# AND THE FIRE SPREAD

             In case the world
changes, in
case things stampede im-
patiently into view/all
arms expectant and the arcade
slings through plasticity an awed spell/in
case this is legible and we are lucky and present not
nearly asleep/not still in the
*after you've gone*/in case
lesions open and the manifest swells to be copied—

                              *"everything that comes*
*my way becomes a picture for me*
*of what I am thinking about at the time"*—

                                        bride
wrapped in rags doused with kerosene
goes enflamed into dusk
drawing the long fog
after her into waters where

                      *of hope/of rapture*
*against a distinction/in traveling/with nothing*
*for eternity/in ambush/for one/in the hope*
*of an endless/of capture/of song/for a stranger*
*in the midst/to a certain/on it/to whom/to whom*
*to a doubt/of being/of guilt/in the tree*
*in the valley/of triumph*
*with lessening/for an excuse/of nails*
*for two sticks/of how/fallen into/of kisses*
*on her lap/to the future/in my shoes/out of spinning*
*for the same/with my stuff/of a morning/to this*

                                   what is
keeps custody of what we will never be
clustered radically in knots
withheld as lateness or shine, its

webbed course stayed. Nothing speaks so there is no
poetry there, just
riot and tidal wisps
blown into shade
and other sham effusions
                              (except when otherwise
alone, although we are now
rhetorically cold, flimsy
as gloves left on a doorstep)
                                                    do not, even then,

agree.


*"For the clarity that we are aiming at*
*is indeed complete clarity, which means that the*
*problems should disappear completely.*
*The real discovery is one that gives peace, that*
*no longer brings itself into question. We*
*demonstrate a method by examples*
*and the series of examples can be broken off."*


All is contained in the bubble's floating code,
not this sheltering skin
with its abrasions.
The lovely conduct of things—architectural, denuded—
seen from above, is elsewhere conditioned
but open to surmise. Here,
in the throat's watery plume, a voice
is besieged by the moon's portrait, mistress
of the huge marquee where the dots are not connected
and of the curve's tree, the river's city, its theme
drawn into a bowl as color's allegiance.

Three doves perch against a plaster sky.
Lichen steal from tapestries and maps.
A pewter flood.


                        What is the world
if not brilliance tarnished to memorible debris?
Toothless, repugnant, Our Lady of Hags
drags from coast to coast her burlap bag

leaking. *O moon!* we call, *O bright thing!*
Who are we to arrest serendipity
when your radiance
dribbles into the sea? The captain's skill
did not save the crew, flaws
foiled passage so what was expected
did not arrive on the stainless steel tray.
Something axiomatic or idiomatic
flew out of the cuckoo's mouth and away
into the century we can almost see.
Huge calipers moved against wind,
doses of prior delight, suds 'n tubs,
gleeful memoirs of an awful age.
Stoic vouchers, burdens of proof—

                              Meanwhile,
a vanguard carried
estrangement into the path of our alliance, and
pandemonium's tryst skyrocketed into the voyeur's polished lens.
Tools of trade. A fashion for linen
sheathed our hands, legs, heads
into fake burdens; bleach
made our eyes smart with revision.
Confidence thus augmented, even the wind
seemed irresponsible—no vacancy at the empty inn
*and the fire spread.* Dissertations multiplied
into the quixotic chat of the living dead,
figurines conversed on rooftop gardens
like balconies of gods. *Tear here; cut along*
*this edge.* Above a broken cauldron
something wept
staining the windows with filigrees of ash.

Caprice in the name of following when nothing, as nothing,
beckons, although our service is still best,
sending the mediated village gruel.
If you, in tawdry remembrance, lamp-lit, were
to come in at last
would you still carry a tune? How long
before the mood comes to rest as in an earlier now

preserved as curious mirth? *What is it?*
Paper umbrellas collect distant rain.
This close to failure
a runt god might flip out of the drain
to rescue us. Tiny gold hip flask; atomic
cufflinks. And that president's grin
never to be endured again
in any language. What's in store for us today,
what catalogue, what bequest? Curtains
spill out onto the sky to hide
a cast of strangers: no machine, no team, no
fat white shoes with good arch support,
just the cold noise of the eternally unhomed.

She gazes from every glossy page,
a slender emptiness. How many stairs
has she climbed to nowhere?
Morning, then, is a mask? And these songs, they?
Toys to prevent vertigo.
Tell me a really scary story, catch this
wild mimosa ball plucked from Blake's reel
(Have you practiced your absence today?)
or some twist of fate the scavengers provide
to tool the future as patterns of wind
braid *the last person to be executed in Florida*
*was a black slave* with the news.
Take heed. Safety in numbers is a hoax.
One man's guide is another's
mistranslation, stumbling
barefoot down the cliff
into the cartoon's inky crawl.
                              *Of its own success*
*upon the asylum/of course/into something/for*
*repressively/of patients/to five or six hundred*
*of that sort/on the edge/on all sides*
*from the semantic/against moral treatment/with it*
*by a growing population/of an organic*
*of the twentieth century/in understanding/by contrast*
*of decay/on their part/in institutional*
*of an infectious illness/of sanity/into some fun.*

Devotional excess laminates the seal.
Facsimile's burlesque obscures the song.

How unseemly our ambassadors.
Could not relax. Could not pull loose.

I carry my skyline with a harsh tip,
an old-fashioned fountain
held by spirits even
after the funeral, so the monastery's sink
is in the center with a logic
behind birds. The birds are necessary
if the dawn is to be useful.
And the enemy suddenly from city to city
comes forward toward the lover
with a frame, an animal, and finds a way
by touch through the drawingroom into the field
pressing down the fire escape by flashlight—

Traipse from island to island with nothing to sell.
Head back to the cabin's shade.

Do it. Leave here. Take your
empirical tirade with you, its
grandeur as winter and zigzag prow,
missing person's voice.
Even in gossip's vacant lot
there's a trace of us in every buyout.

*Of a person/in profile*
*of space/toward you*
*of floors/to live/between/from a box*
*with gold/of a bird/of a man/of its oracle*
*into different/of a content/between objects*
*of an ideal.*

       My hands
in the shape of a house.
Where's the kitchen, where forbearance?
Lost antecedents, faces in another century
when photography is not allowed.
Sell the groom his trousers.

Then I recalled that his buttons
were but partial moons,
and the waterwheels in the cellar
became extinct, or so we are told.

Not in the room with the fake hair's
baleful expertise, not
where the sister is
in the parapet's transition
that others cannot hear, not
the imperious yank
into hoodlum's fame where delusion accrues,
not the hum's drag across limelight
where company is sometimes kept
as tidal mirrors break light.
Could we say this green is humorless
and shines only to please,
an acrobat's poised flip?
Is the postcard delirious
with its orphaned stamp—you go
your way, I'll go mine—the evening
uncollected, a penny on the street?
What is unfinished is not by choice,
gathering inconvenient slang
to ride the large dark over the dark city.
I can see this thing opening onto another thing
but I cannot pronounce it,
neither the one with the frieze of antlers
nor the one with the clocks. Taking off gloves
is a theatrical event, like tossing a pail of water
at an immense flame
or following a script in which a boy
impales himself on a mast as the crowd watches.
The crowd always watches.

*On the walls/in the starkest/in the wrong*
*with our physical/of fire/on fire*
*to the Hebrews/of plans/of sins*
*without the/in this century*
*in a revelation/on the other hand/in this century/to a*

*perception/at least/for a moment/for us*
*in which/of the relation/from the great/between*
*surfaces/of experience/in every/of their*
*to their diction/to each/between surfaces*
*in a forward/from which/by myself/into my innermost*
*by my soul's/with love/in a region*
*with my eye/above my mind/before the light*
*with love/into an awareness/with love*
*from you/in time/out of which features*
*for forces/of something/by mismanagement/from his face*
*of information/on the soundtrack.*

# SEVEN SONGS FOR JOE

1.

Already the air

has no sleeve.
The top and bottom

are charmless.
And the turn, already,
into

an array

concealed
or skipped over

where June was.

Already the stair

is awash
with cherries is

a sled
on rocks.

2.

In the bin below Athens
a trove
broken into shards

        the signed figured
        vase has
        value

stored in tins
cisterns

Dionysus is drinking/the Macedonians
wore this hat

a mixture of wine
and water

vats
large vessels
amphorae

a common object
it has less value
when it loses its context

the deposits are closed
the nucleus is abandoned

the messy debris
under Athens.

3.

In a list of fires:
world fire, world fire II
fire in America
vestal fire
Gondwana fire
Burning Bush.

4.

There is
a
button on
the rug there
is
a button
on the rug
there
is a
button

on the rug
there is a
button on the
rug. Rug.

5.

Halloween eve/walked

under the moon

        jumping

    how now
shed
  Armani mask
        dredged

into black
hound's tooth
rain.

Vintage epicurean knot knows no
spindle, no thread

homespun
comes down, dips

      in the pond's palm        broken

          handle of vase
          splash of stars

                pours out

and
over there the herald is
still golden, recently
returned from his contract
and the natty author

and the tan.
Beautiful young men
are brought forward
extending their flesh
and
and
are told
to listen to the humdrum
catastrophic
street.
Day into night
colder by inches
and
those who are told
start to sing.

6.

A ring is in the wilderness.
It is divorced.

              In the pavement
stonily clad, excluded
from a hand.
Trammel of a carriage, of
wheels without nerve tracking the path

whose entire
makes itself memory

                              come back! come back thief!

vagrant ring
bent into
leftover silvers, wild pearls, foraging needles, print, petals

                    ungathered

                              an immense yellow hauls

its timetable
across a day's
naked throat

combs
fall from the sea

bees
nest in mud.

In the first place
there was no Radio City
no recalled stuff
no Cadillac
no wife Marie.
This passionate loam ebbtide sensation
wasn't it swift?

Boy leaning on brick
the goddess exploding
the ample ruin in the yard.

Now instead a doctrine
of old twilights cast
into our river
scrolls with fevered lists

subtracted

and a glider alights
on far-off sands, its

wings'

incandescent rattle
as the narrative staff
presses its period
(in binding fortune) away.

7.

You with a garden at your feet—lilies
and small red roses, iris—all
out of season in glass vases
on steps

      as if

you had said

it is enough
not to have desire
but for how the day folds out

small napkin
on a wide table

                 we will unwed our sisters

graduate
into little anarchies of dawn

so sham
there will be

only replicas.
What shall we do with the day?

*in memory: Joe Brainard*

136

# MISSING AGES

1.

At times dry weight shifts vicariously on mental limbs like music
hurting remotely.

At times, fathers die and die, but
biography is a false persuasion.

Inhaling the night I am stitched to you
with incendiary sorrow.

A party? In costume, you say, and
invited to dwell in a sea of lords and ladies?
Quit smoking? Weep?
And those magnolias, are they
part of the wall, or of the rushing river
with its vestal gashes arriving on a whim of connective tissue, on air?

In a foreign land we will learn some songs.
They will last as long as the next gold rush.

2.

                        This is my résumé. Hire me.
I am from January, where the winds are severe.
I am an immigrant from evening, hire me.
My father was a sweeper of secrets, a silk merchant
in Vienna, he had no boots, he had no lotion for his skin.
Hire me. This handkerchief is woven from ninety percent.
My daughters are in Mexico on a jaunt. They have not
read of the insurrection, they
do not get CNN. This is my black scarf. This is my painting of a jar.
Hire me. This is a photo of my husband
taken when he was a young man in jail.
I still remember sex, I can tell you stories
of such women you will invite me to your trial. The snow
stinks of yellow. Someone in a corner says thank you repeatedly.
Hire me. I am what you do not know and will not miss.

3.

The rapacious sky is as a winged figure
flaunting its rapture, a film
of film whose beginning middle and end
we will never see. Knowledge is form.
Wait for me under the apple tree on the blue sand.
A discordant glue travels into courage, and the cut
speeds along the finger's edge. Weather
confounds our dreams, we wake humid
with what we forgot while those who stay late
sleep in the margins, fools
for fools' gossip. Millions are spent
on regular episodes from that life.
Starved monks subsume an awful
delay, snowbound, iconoclastic, their
amnesia intact. I was a gallant trooper
thru the history of Nordic exploration,
I sank heavy water.
I wear the soiled increment
as a shield; my eyes break day by day
in sublime iteration: unbearable choice among peers.
We speak in tongues, yes?
All instances fill and empty as
the suction of love plays that rule, coming to stay
in the habits of an angel skinned by disbelief.
He raises the issue to emblematic stature:
nature loves a plague as much as a rose.


4.

The mutant veracity of almost.
The steep incline of a heart.
The dotted line of convention.
The little afterlife of hazard.
What spills from the mouth of a passionate dog.
The voice of reason, its ineptitude with layers.
The amulets of thieves; grief as such.

The occasion purloined.
A brother's best scarf.
A brother's gray scarf.
Between best and gray, an analogy.
Icon of an ordinary okay.
Between nine and fine.
The makeshift bed.
The national interest.

5.

Which from among these absences will you choose?
When the French girl arrives, no one will answer the phone for a week.
If I were invited to sleep over, I would bring
my dowsing rod, over which
you could say your prayers, but if we
touch the beautiful soul it will
never stop raining.
One by one, we are announced, and our
names are a weightless carriage.
Hire me. I live on the stairs. I go up and down.

*to Kenward Elmslie*

# HARM'S WAY, ARM'S REACH

1.

Things are not cured by resilience.
*Thrash thrash* wept the amputated limb
unable to lean, starved of its hair.

A group of men
wanted to avenge
to truncate the city/to make everyone
scream.
            On the bateau, in wild heat
children laughed through the history lesson
through the great façades in the Year of Friendly Fire.

The friend looked away
subverting fate
               (because of the wound)
saying *I disapprove of*
*the personality of the street*
*which cannot be arranged. Henceforth,*
*two out of three curtains must be closed.*

In fiction's unhinged seat
in the hesitant new

resting under a shadow
unbodied in febrile need

and from afar, far in that land
song of the first bird

pressure in the throat
gospel devoted to mercy

a zone or hinge
out of the discursive enclosure

long frieze of furious goddesses
wrath of the drunken boy

in the Home for Depraved Girls
in the Department of Recent Arrivals.

2.

                                My name is an unsolved
equation I come toward you
                        I ask you to meet me
at twilight in the unfinished part of the story
in the small grotto in the room with giraffes
and a man with a string
                            when it is raining
when all the maps are spread on the desk
where the towels/where the nest fell


                                    I write to you
from the place of habit but today I am young
I am merely a slant perpetually drawn
into spelling
            My name is a tall man
who walks along the Street of Books
in the Year of the Mouth who has not forgotten
how to kiss

The friend says
*But in order to fix it*
*you must have a sense of prior perfection* she says *light beauty fire* I say
*toward* and *rage of the weed* and *etymology* and *starvation*.
I say the change or revolution that does not produce
the conclusion or final event

                            catastrophe as definition
                                the wall that was.

3.

Where we come from
abides as choice

it is the way of avowal.

Have you remembered to take all your belongings with you?
Today all distance is summer.

If you open the curtains you will see
the evil wires the broken lock the rifles
the plot
            dark crevices of diminished weight
the lesson of the open hand your mother's maiden name.
You will hear
               a cluster of pilgrims undaunted by speed
flagrant as any transparency
the indelible scheme of the wish
a parade for no reason

                    an apricot thud where the limb was.

# ASHES, ASHES
# (ROBERT RYMAN, SUSAN CRILE)

1.

Humped gravity/tree-backed vatic shard/white
disarray/arc
                    secretly allied to the dark clear dark/herald
sick of his forms, dry
with remorse.

There is a cup in the landscape buried under the indefinite
as if it would last: salt, sugar, salt.
Sooner or later he'll want a child
hushed up against him
spawned in egregious thirst. Pale
inventory of a lunar smile/applause track
slips off the rails, flute twisted, strings
knotted and loose. Must be numbers, letters,
afloat on the surface: augur, thread, mast,
honeycomb, terrace.

I am jealous of his garment, his shirt's wide cut,
gaudy transience crouched in his throat,
great thimble of heat poured out—

a thing in the landscape:
salt, sugar, salt.

2.

Now this news.
If you do not mention it she will not cry.
I laughed as well at the child's invention.
Yesterday I saw a painting
of a young woman in a red dress. Yesterday

yesterday I saw
paintings of fire. I met a woman she said

*my father my father my father*
and as she spoke he became her portrait.

If a room is artificially white
all whisper in the affirmed
physical space: scraps of
touch touching touch.

The violinist moves
like a marionette/his
legs buckle/hair
jumps with light/torso

breaks forward.
Music adheres
enclosing the figured silence
as if setting were bondage.

As if setting were bondage
and we on the brink had walked up to it/raw thread
chafing the waters of the percolating wave.
As if we could say to the fire,

*Stop! I command you, stop!*

3.

That night the moon was the Evil Banana King
crouched in a bowl.

See, said the child, drawing the light,
this is The Princess I asleep on her bed

this her pet snake/this
is the mother in her slip
she is wearing a nest on her head
she is a long lady standing in front of a leaky mirror
she says I would rather be in jail than
hidden in these devotions

I am making red and yellow stitches
although my crayons are stale.

Now she is walking toward a cave
where the tools are hidden and the Book of Instruction,
peeled into slight wings, batters the foam.

This is a circle.
The name of the circle is Gray Pond.
There are lilies on the pond/you cannot see them
as if the memorial had rubbed away.

This is the ghost.

4.

This black thing is a mistake.
It could be a cat or a cart.

It is lonely like a mouth in a desert
under sand. I

do not know who hears it.
I do not know who calls.

It is a long way since
with no way out into a song.

There is an ecstasy in battle,
on the somber chasm's edge.

That thou wouldst narrate me
thru these worlds.

I am in derelict garb
my category is broken

I covet the extreme.

5.

Then the periphery dawned as later, as ebb tide
on a channel, as the gray pond of recognition,
the memorial rubbed into a wall.
How soon? you ask, and again, How soon?
You may as well ask is the water bloody
is the chair frail.
           And, at the horizon, a ribbon of fire
finds its way to the woman's dress to ravish it so in the box
wild ashes fly about in a litter of silence.
The father-woman and the child do not meet, the
violinist never smiles. Is it merely a sunset, this fire,
seen from the dusty window of a passing train, or is it
the oiled conflagration of an event brought home to us as a trophy:
which comes first, artifact or source,
and what stroke stokes the flame?

# IN THE MUSEUM OF THE WORD
# (HENRI MATISSE)

1.

There was the shield of another language
transient enclosure/gate
                               swings open
shut shut
           walking unnoticed into it
                           as with *avec*
down stone steps into the vineyard
               rose as decoy/beauty as use
         riding up onto the surface
                   glance, sway/hawk
comes down dragging silence with it
no light, no applied Sun King
                      opposing shine, commonly
                    bereft
                            creature of habit lost in a wood.

Here I said take these thimbles these hooks
you can count them and toss them away
one six nine/they
will fit under any stream, fill any slot
will color the waters
of the restless exhibit
                  lizard's billowing throat
        hiccups on a wall/its tongue
        flicks air
                        bird-strewn wind.

And the milkman's doubling dream, his
dilemma, the composition of his
intolerance for dawn/great
Aubergine Interior too frail to move: link
between A Conversation and event. There was

there had been an awkward tour.

I was shown two rivers, their vistas

                                    snailfooted/waterskinned abyss
                                    wheelwinged staring at muck
                                    weedy, indifferent, purplepronged up
                                    in avid rays their comprehensive *is*
                                    bearing emblems smaller than time

under the decor
coiled among rocks

I met a woman with odd eyes
she said this is the figure of guilt
hurling a snake boulder
                        wall
ripped from a wall
                                        fragment installed.
This country is a
cavern of drunk light/shade rubbed onto day
the corpse is not luminous/vines dangerous/flowers profuse
as in an arbitrary Eden. These
consolations also are damaged/seepage under roofs
thru which the musics
might come.

2.

She traveled.

Sun lay against her knees printed on purple
boughs fell with a thrash
color collected on the dusty sea floor
                        fronds meticulously scissored/commerce
            raged thru the sky binding its harmonies
regardless of space.

Although something insisted, pointing.
Although similar doors did not open similarly.
Blackbirds reminded her of written blackbirds/it was
humid with blackbirds/her mind an inscription/a proverb

or heap, so she could almost see its faithful
retrieval: monkey hanging with long limbs/bird
on her shoulder/rigid man/moon
doubled in glass.

3.

A fable of prescience/looking up into the sky's garden
and the statues on the roof
withstanding bombardment

        seven paces to Paradise
           halted startled voyagers/nothing to correct
             the possible direction collides with the way
               each morning's tray a rudimentary splendor.

I said here are some useful numbers
some untranslatable rain

        façades pockmarked in the new contingent state
         now untethered on the Street of the Harp
          the blind man cannot/soft sloped palm
           dog leading him on into the unscented garden

They are scooping out the bloods in jars
the real has a stench/it is not
the tableaux we elicit.

I went up a steep hill in a foreign country
in unknown grass/there was an aperture
        boats, birds
             many unknown letters
           snake-wrapped sphere
                  Persephone delayed
                   stolen, raped
Hotel where Mozart stayed/street where Brecht
Beckett's daily walks

         impermanent oracular trace so that
*not any fragment will do* counting my steps

from margin to margin/scenic on foot
turning a page.

4.

In Museum Street, Liu Hai is
standing on a three-legged toad

the toad
was thought to inhabit the moon

it lost its leg
in order to correspond

with the three-legged bird
that inhabits the sun.

*And the Apostles were fishermen and thieves*
*base fellows neyther of wit nor worth*

     seal
   reduced to a wax turd
    flaunting a tail
        charred Charter's remains
         under glass

Merlin
helps a young man
to paint his
shield/an illustration

Attendants in a garden mounted on a crane

Under green and ochre glazes
under turquoise purple and ochre glaze
with aubergine, green and straw glazes

In a woods a black scroll
let us caption the first scene

on oak on oak on oak
on poplar on lime

green earth has been used under gold leaf
instead of the usual orange bole

*as well as I can*

      As if conducted to the eulogy fields to lie down with a shade
      under turbulent vines
      walls studded
      Piero's meticulous plumage

Come this way said the guard this is where
your opponent lies grieving
here are the spoils set in violent maps, re-
named, disinhabited, inherited, made
bloodless with shine.

Read this example
it praises the country of origin

it teaches you facts
in the new gray wing

                lion, corpulent monk

Here are some postcards to send home/the one
you want is sold out/the thing you came to see
is temporarily gone

                that she is seated/that the door
                that the window
                that she wears part of a tree
                that the color of the conversation
                moves as if it were sky/that the frame
                continues to dissolve
                (sadness of the Rose Marble Table)
                man wearing a pajama column
                rigidly pronounced/woman
                redrawn in response—

                *Is it possible to memorize this blue?*

                *to Thomas Neurath*

# WHEN COLOR DISAPPOINTS
# (JOSEPH BEUYS)

1.

Something must have lifted our spirits
caused our tongues to be untied
dreamed us from ruin
where the ur-bells begin

                                        sun
roiled under an elk's body
penciled toward or into its subject
willing to aspire

as the turbulent same
doubles its augur     *"body color"*     *"blood"*

These (unnamed, above)
have a gash or surprise, a smile
missing the dangling thing as the tacit
crosses over to where meanings are

                                        mind
changing again into its mystery
flume of song and cedars made to weep
across from the flags in the signature gardens

trajectory of a fragment at all times in view

          —meet me in the designer collection
          —there's a limit here how white is your hair?
          —are you, were you ever, afraid?

*Tulipe noire* and fat stain
below street level in the currency of paper

                    wrinkled ribs of light
                    bi-coastal war

cross retrieved from snow
boy listening for red, hearing its cure

Partita of leaves
as a desire for evidence, heroic esplanade
of the remnant museum, so the morbid thing
anchors a panoply of *yes,* including
a swan

Something must have diverted our pain

*This painting has been re-*
*moved during the re-*
*hanging of the Second Floor Lounge Please*
*excuse the vacant space it will be re-*
*placed as soon as possible*

Grammar of Lincoln's eyes
bi-weekly take-home essays

Speaking from within a secret
filament dissembling, the tongue's
ardent, literal wish

calendar awkwardly re-
newed: old field, old damage

said to come true as any interlude must.

2.

In a further stripe  iconoclast mode  which
jiffy to                    roiling haphazard thing
from        All these beginnings
printed askew, a pattern
quietly revealed over insurmountable  Sense
closes over what   to be
                    heavy                on film.
The motel's windows open onto a hall of
onto an American            all predecessors

                    native tile. I have come
          these names, as to say, these
preferences, one shore over                    one
skeletal phrase                         emulating
its hearer.


Something withstood?
Something shattered?


How crowd
          off into  lent forsythia
raging    the fill  anonymous
               rank the blinking obscene
as
       the committee in absentia.
                                        Now
mirrored
bricks do travel      schemes
                                   rest in the archive. Some
thing stamps on the screen. It matters
less in another language
                             captured, reproduced as
in space.


The classic range incalculably slit.


Old zero range to which nothing comes back.
Later, when doubling ceases, lines,
spells, whatever. So the earth has its day,
phantom chant, surf. Such
listening requires ammunition: a brag, an
apology, syntactical praise. Something roots
the sound's principle, rinsing lesions
recorded by evening        insects,
other dry apparitions unthwarted by grass.


3.

An avenue of wool, karate, gap
hectic magics swell into magnolias

gracefully aloft
                    head of a woman
posing for it, vehemently caught
the incursion stilled thus—
autonomous migrant persons
retained as sight


                    And the arriving spectacle
reflected as half of any width
mountains of calls whose voices are not
not rain, not music, not the deed recalled
not any *is* filtered through joy.

Completing the fragment, lasting that long.

                              So assume the perdition of
answers, asking the clock
now trailing after his vestments

responsibly repressed, dare to conceal
the way girls are said to, weaving shadows
into flesh, refuting his stare

so the motif is instructive
borrowed from
the universal real

gesture true to itself
leaf or stroke

                    ugly gold-like thing
                    shuttering bough.

4.

I have imagined something urgent is happening
imagined I am awake

I recall the bitter neon kingdom
patina of sentient beings, reversal of gloss

I think his fingers touched this fat book
where all secrets are told

man off to an assignation
woman in wait

I think his ears hear
blame on the radio

a bit of thunder recorded in another country
news of a solo     The instruments she makes have
extremely long    thirty or
                              played by rubbing the hand along extremely long
resonances    I    it is a pleasurable excursion

I have come to see
your ladder, cane, hat
the tear at the back of your knees
your name that belongs to others
so I say it not to you

the falling motif of the twilight
bells, many bells
some were bells
they may have been bells.

*to Paul Shullenberger*

156

*From*

# CLAMOR

*(1991)*

*There I cannot find There*
*I cannot hear your wandering prayer*
*of quiet*

—SUSAN HOWE

*So silence is pictorial*
*when silence is real.*

—BARBARA GUEST

# TUSCAN VISIT (SIMONE MARTINI)

1.

Day leaned from its agency: a false, hollow gold,
an old temporary bridge, huge trees
bunched over the night like night bunched
into another language—
                            leaned, and sifted
its warnings onto her.
It seemed to ask
why carry these figures on your back
why adhere when feet have already blossomed
on the slippery tile, and the carved faces
look down, hidden and humorless because sacred.
That day was a little stung, a little ruined.
The girl had brought the weather with her
like a toy blindly churning a smoky stench
into the coiled trees. Yellow hedges,
pruned into steps, where no one walked,
where everyone had walked, were a riddle or task
something in any case to enter willingly
as one passes into sight. The statues glared.
The bridge rattled like gunshot briefly, under pressure.
She thought of the voice she knew best and heard it arch
from side to side, stitching a canopy.
She could look nothing up.
She could only guess.

2.

It must have been early
before light had split her unfinished skin of dream
and awakened the tumbling arc of saying—

                In Siena, a sloped shell
         choreographed to wander/to sleep/to kiss
         to run freely across/to be sheltered
         to eat/to watch/to talk—

*Who is it?*
It must have been early,
the ground newly splintered into grass,
sitting on the porch, reading,
sparrows stringing from limb to limb; early,
at dusk, swallows looping, long columns of gnats,
bats pinching the air, dogs yapping in the courtyard,
the breeze breaching her ankles
draped in the foreground, cool smoke
lifting from the frame
a white scent
in which gold weather sat with gold birds
depicting it—
*Who is it?*

3.

A conspiracy of stars, night's umbilical blue
shunt—details—shunt—
looking at and being in
*Have you seen my diary?*
*What time is it?*
She twists away from her book—
what did she see?
The hills as a journey,
the sky as a sign,
cypress beards—
it came as a subject
lick, stamp, address
she twisted away
shunt—details—shunt—
and stared
and startled
*disquiet, reflection, inquiry, submission, merit*
looking at and being in
a conspiracy of blues, night's umbilical star.

4.

Detained in such an arena, mute, subjected,
consumed by what she could not know,

the trance of facts surrounding her,
codes among the multitudes—
*Would you save my place?*
Flies, bees, birds
and the harbor full of boys
sporting their nudity under other auspices,
her love engraved like a platitude
on a charm, even her solitude—she

hears the crest of bells
through the patient door
dividing her from it, it from us—
inspired, installed, ceded.

5.

You go to a place, you stare
at the weather, naming it fondly.
You are amazed by the moon.
You say *portal* and *garment* to yourself
and notice the pressure of young fat thighs
invested in satin. The trees
ride in and out of the composition
and the hills, frescoed to the sky,
are absorbed and absorbent in milky light.
You pluck stray flowers; you drink local wine.
You go to a place, you see
a woman trimmed in gold;
the women are trimmed in gold
and are not transparent.
You say to yourself *spine.*
You say *kneel, issue, wing*
as the map flies open into its depictions.
Her hand on the cowl of her robe,
her small mouth turned down,
her thumb holding a book open,
her body recoiled from the offered lilies.

# GESTURE AND FLIGHT

1.

She could be seen undressing.
That is, in the original version
she could be seen undressing

A red jacket
across a white chair

At first she had needed a coin,
a shelter, marriage, and these
led quickly to her doubt

*"feminine" "visceral"*
quoted rudely

which then fell rudely
through a ring and into her chamber
where she could be seen undressing

a gesture, a glance
so the thing stood for its instance

folded tidily under the lamplight
with the logic of fact.


In another instance, a volcano
is hidden in the distance, a triangular hood
under the sky's usual pan
and unusually adept clouds
but the image on the stamp is cloudless.

In yet another, masculine, version,
an arc intersects process
as ribbons of color are technically masked
so as not to bleed / her jacket
falling off the chair as she turns, her mouth /

the gesture of the brush exploited, willfully exploited:
*"volition" "deceit"*. And the girl's own story
includes shoes, bottles, beds,
a jacket, hair

Then both or all sexes
foregather under the island's moon
without so much as an announcement from the captain
*We are experiencing a turbulence* telling us
what we already know. Already lovers
are rowing across the inlet
as the moon rises.
Let us hope there is no photograph of the event.


2.

A half-finished sensuality?
Bloom, opiate
                    *No*
The partial locale of things?
Residence, place
                    *No*
The ardor of the provinces?
Well, how was Italy?
                    *No*


Spun from an initial prop—
avoid the *the*—
so here goes this part—
wound into what looks like—
Family romance! Caprice plus longing equals?
Vessel! Accoutrement! Awakening!

Wake up!
Is the map a puzzle or the puzzle a map?
The sun is not an earring. The moon is not its mate.
Each variant shuffles into view or is shot
through the hole where the button was
on colder mornings, and cloth
is pinned to the wall with neon pilings.

Hardly a story yet and yet
plot must be the succinct
restored to its aftermath.
Turn her slowly, her here, ere he

Eerily, sun comes through as time, and I'm
found in its provenance: trees and such and *plish,*
wet polish over old boards where he and she stand
among arresting branches, their countless
one and one and one. A picture? A map?
They must hear air moving among broken anomalies of air,
its chant revived in the actuality of their needing it:
hymnal, not critique, nothing to touch, to see, to eat.

That would be flight
but this, a ripped adventure
in tandem's everlasting grip, also
is subject to song: so go on
up the tune's horizon, up, up, up
its prohibitive curl, snarl, smile
almost as visible as

if only air could carry such inferences,
if things could be thusly sung,
an option of partial seeing
and of plentiful response

each iteration—
tentative plow, wild new damage—
moving from stranger to stranger
tracing, as if, an intimacy.

Ice doth hand stiffly.

3.

What were those kisses made of
and those tissue-clad children
their remnants laid across the hills like fog?
Had she danced in the temple where the Egyptians lay?

Had they? They was the city's ruse
to keep us moving from station to station
hoping for chance to erupt
from the dangerous crux of endings.
There is a list and everyone is on it.
But to be turned toward a discrete, raveled flame
composed of the foreground, lasting only as long as passage—
could nearness ever suffice?
In this version, she takes a screen from its window
and air is relentless,
a rhythmic presentation of toward,
as the foggy grid subtracts to its object,
the object to its pile. Certainly,
she could be seen undressing
as she stretches her arms overhead
as she touches her shoe.

*to Peter Straub*

# THE FRENCH GIRL

1.

Someone plays
               & the breaking mounts.
Raw material for worthy forthcoming;
indecipherable, discrete.
                   Plays
rhapsodies as the air cools
and vanquishes: nothing sits still, yet.
The land is a result of its use, I explained.
Everything else rested while the kids made a girdle
removed from classical syntax. Shed, and

something breaks, mounting
the small hill to its vista: I saw
a rope of trees in another country.
I could not say *I am lost* in the proper way.
The season is huge.
This house is haunted: I planted it.
Where? In the shed, and

spoiled by attention. You see?
Every bit counts, when the morning displays
the serious ratio of the given stars.
What made us tear the hours into lines?
So things became a burden to shed, and

astute as a hungry pilgrim
but not brave, not expert.
It is impolite to stare. Is unwise
to plunder the easily forgotten,
easily shed, and

2.

They drummed and drummed, attached to a vestigial
clamor. The heat splayed; sparklers
ravished the fog.

Morning tore the dead back to shore;
enemy ships floundered and were forgotten.
Still, nothing was appeased:
the living silhouette drifted into view
like an ephemeral sail promoting ease
between wreckages.
                              Not speaking a word of English
she animated the landscape
with abundance, a chosen self
freely translated into the color of her eyes.
Awkward and luminous, a stilted charm
separating figure from ground, and solving it.
What pushed up toward the abysmal
with such new appraisals, such sure interest?
The mute girl had seen glories
but what had she come to know?
A finite figure in a rainy field.
A naked figure in a pool.
A skipping figure across a bridge.
A lost figure on a city street.
A moaning figure on a huge bed.
A smiling face in a photograph.
All summer, I circled the garden for her sake.

*In memory of my sister Jennifer*

# TRIBE (STAMINA OF THE UNSEEN)

1.

What estranged methods, what original repose.
The entailing ground, flat and firm enough,
is littered and agreeable—to which, to which
our own selves trail, hauling.
The wild cannot call.
Things are covered with paisley and stain.
Estranged and original, the system of recovery
is still unknown as what is perceived
proceeds to the near at hand.
                                    A stage, an address.
A willingness to submit to an interview: like to unlike.
Were we to permit this, were I to permit us,
that room would sail into open domain: there
where the farms have settled.
Hauling, as from elsewhere,
and crafted now into mild or bitter climates,
their shapes loaded into the sentence, molten,
resembling maps. As each ends, another gains its forebears,
angling into the emulsion as a need to be present.
The bride tries on a gown.
Rain lets fall its expedient veil
listing its terms, less known, less coherent,
than the troth of difference.

2.

Permitting us, I cannot tell how marvels are broken
or what dispersals settled back into the common life.
Here the bitch comes in an aftermath of identity
thinking herself memorable, having saved best for last.
That she is cold is irrefutable (the bride, the veil)
eyes fledged from the immodest glare of regard,
limbs accurately hungered. So we huddle
on the distressed, inarticulate streets
for as long as it takes
before we lift from the denuded shelf
its harvest.

Someone moans through thin walls
between the sonata and football game, the new room
fully achieved, listening for acquittal.
The blessing is ugly, unless you are there
for the final, blissful throb.
Tucked into the encounter
as the flip side of excess, boredom
turns to passion, passion
to the closed glossary of events mimicked here.
A child might come along
singing and radiant, sweetly adrift
on the wind's prow. She is a proposal.
She is uncensored, but for the conditions.
She quits the visible, a defiant intersection of modes,
heaved, unstuck, estranged and original, saying
*I am the issue. I am what you promised to do.*

# CLAMOR

1.

It was a trance: thieves, clowns, and the blind girl
passed symmetrically under the wide structure
as a floor passes under a rug.
Was this enough to go on, this scrap?
Had I entered, or was I pacing the same limits:
the room brought forward to another landscape,
its odd birds, its train, its street lamp
stationed like an unmoving moon. At night, the cries
assembled into the ordinary speech of lovers before love
as the train pulled up the space, passing and passing.
Were these categories to be kept—thief, clown, blind girl—
or were they too narrowly forensic, too easily found,
the whining insatiable drift insufficiently modeled.
They were an invitation to appear, appease, applaud,
in short to respond, be magical.
In the old days, we howled.
In the old days we chanted our lists until they
were deciphered, lifted the leaves, touched the broken clay,
counted the steps quickly, saying this is the one with the key,
this is the one for whom I will awaken.

2.

Affection is merciless: the wind, the excluder.
So much ruptured attention, so much pillaged from the stalk.
Even the nerves stray from precision, announcing
their stunned subject. Merciless: a field of snow
flying like jargon, sweeping the issue away
in a halo of cold, its purpose
lifted from the flat climate, from its nub or throb.
Lifted on impossible wings we are generous, we dare.
But affection is merciless: the dead in their thin garb
walking the ruined streets, inventing us in stride and envy.
It is said they will make their way
back to us, as what rises saves itself, falls.
What is the speed of this doctrine, what dividends,

what annual yield?
When will he give it back,
when will I laugh in the untidy yard
and when will her eyes, staring at me
because she sees only her departure from me,
see me left here. Further adventure is further delay.
I used to count the days. I do not want to count the days.

# BOY SLEEPING

These difficulties—flamboyant tide, modest red berries,
or modest tide, flamboyant berries—
the moon keeping and casting light
onto the boy's sleeping face
and the posture of his knowledge
erected on the fatal—
                      Is this how it begins?
Or is the solid figure of the night
only a wish to survive the last word said
so that such natural things induce furthering
after the episode of the shut.
Should I tell him his face mirrors the lost?
Should I tell him to wake, marry, find, escape

The ones whose voice exhausts itself on the recurrent
whose fraudulence speaks without images
whose desire spends itself
on indifference, and whose light
makes light of us, those of us whose bearing is
to continue—
                    What is the sublime
but a way, under the pressure of not knowing but caring,
to join the crowd at the slam, to lust openly
for the insecure moment when she turns, not yet dead,
and says: *I am coming with you nevertheless and because.*

I remember when a word
first advanced like a dart at a target,
a star creasing the sky, a lie
told to save the situation while damning it.
I remember when the annual survey included nothing abstract
because the war was full of particulars, particular events.
I remember a ride from the suburbs, sun setting in the windows,
reminding me that I would forget, and so
reminded me not to forget, although
the dead woman in the sleeping boy's face
is a better example.

How much we want to disobey
the sanctity of the kept,
to deny the already as it strides forward
without introduction, revising
before our eyes the unelicited partition of morning.
The precedent of the real mocks us.
Rain spills uncontrollably from above like a test.
Can we follow these new waters
or are we already too fond, our agility mired
in the scripted river rushing under the bridge.
This is asked to keep up going one way or another
lest the pause spread, flooding the field with reflection.
At the center of discourse, forgotten or unnoticed,
a train passes carrying a woman in her youth,
a terrorist, and a boy
waking, wishing he were some place else.

*to Richard*

# OF THE MEADOW

### 1.

*Did you like Switzerland?* you ask for the first time
and motion for someone else to take the wheel.
Trope of what? You are no one's mother,
no one's dauther-in-law
and are not exemplary.

                    What of the meadow?
Lavish, syntactic, new in the natural key
but frugal and obscure in translation.
So you want to put it in a jar
on the mantelpiece to steer us in a direction,
into casual excellence, once wild.
Something about it makes you hurry
before the next one comes along
to render it formal, instructive, true.
You want to be known
as the one who got out from under,
who survived the winter. But
yesterday I heard you say *shredded, dice,*
taking what you could get, like a stranger.

### 2.

Say, *We did not get what we came for*
and proceed to your destination
like a commercial without sound.
You strip away the drama's script
and come to the task refreshed.
Days pass, with rain, with mice
busy in the eaves; another pond nearby.
Engage it to drain or flush
the episode out: kneeling, as children,
against the event, plucking a bloom
from the Chinese screen which, you believe,
later went up in flames. But that could be
only the fatigue of memory washed clean,
bleached, newly ransacked and incredulous

but for its renown, wandering
the upper tier of a proscenium
garbed in quotations, acquisitions,
sheets of white linen already, initially, inscribed.
You tell yourself to wait, say
the actor is the audience, the audience asleep
on a bench in a park in a small city
that the troupe might visit.
The water seems to lengthen in the breeze.
Later, you dream the image, adding time to space,
and someone, correctly, says, *We knew all along*
*that the city was beautiful.* So things
manage to go on in a parade of similarities:
lilies on this pond, that pond.
And the long curtains divide
still touching the shore, the stage, the glass.


3.

On the picr, among the banished,
sealed away from the hot toys
listed on the page as *fable*
our sightseeing continues
like a flock risen from ashes
where the fire stood bequeathed, or stolen.
*Where are the matches?* I had asked, my feet
wet from long grass.
That girl keeps running by the door.
That man keeps asking questions.
You keep saying, in answer to mine,
*No, I am happy.*
                   So I go on coming to it
as to the edge of water,
blind with a fiction of recovery.
Is this what you meant by persistence?
The voice recorded into mimicry,
the water folding light into its surface,
the girl materializing like a path along the ridge.
What are the signs, now
that you cannot correct the impression
as I arrange the flowers, as I notice the incomplete.

# HOW THINGS BEAR THEIR TELLING

They settle out from their curfew
a splash of redemption, a ploy

Steeped in earliness
listening is scenic

Uplifted ruffled boughs
anchor the pond

To be near, tame and graphic
small derivations drawn mutely forward

Footsteps on the pier
quickly dry

His white cuffs open
his collar open

To fuse, conclude, adhere
to dangle and arrange

Along the road, a garden is waiting
along the road, a house will be built

The painter's huge back—
the volume's tent

A celebration among strangers
a bride's opaque face

Where she travels she is
harpoon in the back of a whale

Tinctures, sets, rips—
leaping as conquest, as plot

A mower and an old man's booming voice
a chronology is mislaid

What is palpable is shunted—
the distance between landings

Deep in the foreground like a caress—
the breath draws in

There are these rims
these goggles clouded and abrupt

A narrative resembles a lost ornament
the dying resemble the living closely

Is someone really sawing the night?
Any choice is exclusive

Saying and crickets abide—
they forgot to put up signs

Both dice and sky are loaded—
the night is like Chicago

Seeing through to thought
a nude and voracious stranger

If you are stung, try cool air—
the sun is not a light bulb

Not so much spinning as raking
not so much burning as fleeing toward

Days the size of postcards
voyages along steps

Immediacy precludes reversal—
jumping, he contained her pleasure

To touch, to refrain from touching
nearness is its own, inexhaustible law

A temporal clerestory evades the threshold
no smears, no red ink

Stairs, halls, doors—
an incitement to hurt, to be inconclusive.

# LOCAL BRANCH

The chill impediments—caution, doubt
yoking us again to the clandestine trap

where wonder, like a strange forgiveness,
comes in from the hollow

whose word I had recently
held or clasped, had altered, refused

finally in this round of seeing's belief,
the mind watching itself depart

as the girl I now own, her
pattern of rushing away to escape

that other, less mild convergence
as to a page, a mast, another's insistence.

The warranted came stressed, adoptive,
who was that masked man but an idea

of the eternal, fictive and obscene,
forever transcribed but broken, incoherent.

I told her but first I asked her
to tell me and she told me: this, if not

another, would be this.
Seems plausible, if abhorrent, and so

wisdom came to play against the backdrop.
How does it look? Like a broken—

like wandering from the story, telling it
backwards, telling it in an irretrievable code.

*to Stacy Doris*

# PROM IN TOLEDO NIGHT

A new heat comes up on a grand scale.
Were we waiting for it, as for a link,

ask about sugar? Well, the heat is
here. I thought I would speak of it

for someone to adjust the antenna, to

the recent suburban content, how much
sky is now blocked. I have run into

coolly, as flatly as possible, given

chatted with both florists. Boys have
been born to two nice women: Raphael

numerous persons I know. I have

on a trial basis. I don't know why but
this heat is like a quarry dug into

and Penn. Some friends have separated

omissions, intuitions flying out of the
cranny or slot we thought irreducible,

the side of a hill. Intangible

some things, uninteresting things,
colors, pigs, toys, the usual river.

Earlier, I had written, mentioning

radio: *I saw a good one, it looked like*
*it could run.* That was before the heat

I noted a couplet from a song on the

cabaret. Another poem begins: *"But*
*we were drawn away again by portraits"*

but after I had won the howling dog at the

those who were still living, but who
had forgotten while the violins

pictures where we could be idle against

I don't know what that means. The poem
continues: *"Beautiful faces*

Explained the conditions

It seems someone else was in the room.
This is a Mercury Production.

Turn in the light; the two walk, stop

*Evolving like the slow surge of history."*
That part of the poem ends there, but

And then the spectacle

*room to its original strangeness."* I
Have better things to do with my time,

Then another: *"Restoring a*

I mention it was prom night in Toledo?
Have you noticed how the specific is

now that I am in the city again. Did

continuities of what we want.
                              Of what

always a gash or wound in the ongoing

unraveled speaks for itself, a mask.
I'll stop concluding that desire is

we want to keep, to cure, care for. The

a girl rides from the field in hot sun.
We stopped, once, at a lake to swim

a good place to start. I'll quit, as

the old red Ford. Last night you said
my dreams would improve but

when the heat became intolerable in

*"And after April, when May follows*
*And the whitethroat builds, and all the"*

you were wrong.

on a black table, some around your house,
some around mine, and the specific looms

Peonies weighted, three in a white vase

We turn and turn through always and ever
with *as* between us. When you laugh my

again. In my mind there is a carousel,

the point of entry: the gash on the hill,
what we see as we ride. From the log:

arms feel light. Your voice has become

a small Pa. town. Ducks, chickens, geese,
fresh eggs. I had some bacon, too, I

2:15 is your time. Stopped for lunch in

about that duplicated hill. As I write
*duplicated hill* I look up and the first

never eat bacon or eggs. I'm thinking

the sign says bridge may be icy. My
mind revolves around where and when.

Big hill appears ahead. We walked east.

Trying to describe a miniature calla
lily only makes matters worse, and

passing Presque Isle

I grasp at particulars when I am a
deposit of hermetic, avid cares

proves your point about dimensions

be, found in the radiant furl of skin
as it plummets, seen from under a

whose known qualities could be, might

akin. I can feel the city's nearness,
its less than equal attitude in

cluster of new foliage, or something

my bracelet got hitched to a girl's
sleeve—a frenzy took place around

skirmishes—elbows hit elbows, wrists

Is this a form of exaltation or despair?
I love conjecture, although its stipend,

some running shoes on sale on the street

linear vein pierced, is too delicate.
Interspersed among these less than valiant

day after day of weather reports like a

*"My love, this is the bitterest, that*
*Thou/Who art all truth and who dost"*

innings I'd turn to pure lyric:

among the temporarily stricken; old
litany of passage. Against a glass

*Love me now* . . . warble of language

I've come to see through nothing, ad–
mit to only a haphazard verisimilitude

backdrop and its brilliant flanges

-eyed art. Of course you, as both
occasion and witness, pull me through

similitude of the storyteller's wide

gloss it amuses you to touch. I had
planned to leave earlier, but these

like a thread of feather whose pale

Suddenly the sense of prelude becomes
a hard spray of contingencies,

keep making their mobile shadows

the most essential. She turns to look
into the glass, watches as the image

adamant, refuting, like a tax on

of a gate closing off the garden for-
ever. The model, exposed, could not

expand, shifting to the calamity

with the rest, and nobody would know
how it ended, as nobody had known

last, but would be shredded

briefly wild; a fan eeked its rotations

into an alley; her friend, a girl,

*"I have but to be with thee, and thy hand"*
She reads a line from the open page

told her mildly, obliquely, to rescind.

to increase or ease the new implication.
It was as if a lance, aimed into the night

of a nearby volume, hoping for chance

of a passing stranger who had been surprised
but had remained diffident as he plucked it out

had hit a real target, had stung the arm

He had taken a rag, knotted it,
walked uphill in the direction

and watched as blood poured from the hole

He had asked, handing her back the weapon
This tale boiled up from the flat black earth

from which the thing had come. *Is this yours?*

to breach the destitution of our aimless band's
hungers. The more familiar pattern

one long spring whose sole aim appeared to be

became interesting only when we decided
to participate in it. The room

This habit of one thing leading to another

airless so that she, in it, felt
breathless, reckless, faithless

painted a virulent green, seemed

As I sleep, an unnatural extremity prevails.
I am entrusted to a stranger, harnessed

*"I have but to be with thee, and thy hand"*

a spill I try to prevent like this.
Did you use a cup for the dice?

or yoked while floodgates are lifted

with either the actual or absolute.
In the full heroic flush, we

Am I *A?* Each line is a quibble

How can I keep an even keel: *"Single tree
in brown field: two trees: flashing*

could not be more discerning, note

*empty corrals: white fences: cows:*
*arrows: your fingers: your: small bird*

*on barns: silver: wrists: your fingers:*

*like a beacon: the smell of oats:*
*right lane ends; Merge left: you*

*attacking hawk: shade: that green silo*

*Different hair: your . . ."*
                              Being marked

by the river, those girls with

solitude cheats, it is to you I am speaking
while at the same time wanting a world

as thought: what to suggest, what elicit?

of how it looks but how it is. You
are the constituent object; this distance

others might recognize, not because

                         Others will say
she was just passing the time—

an argument. Against what?

Animal allegiance—makes dinner from scratch
abating or diluting while the last thrash—

a milder form of discourse

The river is nearer. Little conversations
at the checkout counter.

still to be seen against—I am less at ease—

I remember the room I invented you in,
how happily captive I felt in such

At last, a reductive mood

exactitude in this, an idea of being
as being with. This is rudimentary

confinement. There was, and is

say love is an attitude toward difference
in its freest form, adhering, inimical

but festive, if the subject persists

Now, let's leave to the cartographers
while the music lasts, the privileged

to time's jurisdiction. Space for

most intimate, most entailing.
Abundance and loss are the terms.

Information a display, a harbor

the arch or bridge or catapult—
a dart piercing an arm—is how

earn the right to ford the rapids.
That she wants to converse in silence

we redress, reconceive our predicament

the unutterable collapse of particulars
yet speaks its priority and stillness.

is how desire crumbles disbelief

Men skip succinctly over the drawbridge
muscular and vibrant in the distilled age

Pleasure is the cost of time, as may be

some future proverb in which complexity is
soothed: give the infant beer for her tooth.

The women darken with expertise, hum

blooming above the pond in memory. Our task
is to be less defeated by these children

But the fireworks were only partly successful

girl is out of control, she reaps her hunger
on small things, rips handfuls of blooms,

as they shrilly discard the air. The golden

seeing what I contain, as one contains
an ancient song. *La La La,* a spray of notes

rips hair, my only sight, now actually

stick to cloth, home sweet home as awful
as a flood, a crowd, an epidemic beyond halt.

In heat, an absent, singular source. Words

cure for the incommensurate. *La La:* who cares
in the fresh air to which we now, even now,

rapture is the antidote, as may be.

# REMORSE OF THE DEPICTED

Harsh brag of the inexhaustible: *replete, replete.*
Lured away from choice as from extreme devotion.
Another time, friendships will soften
into broader categories, letting gaps heal.
The undoing that ending is
is prettier if less abrasive
so we might come and go in aspects:
I'll keep his face, her hands, your voice
observing the necessary between.
Words cling to other words
as we have seen, although even these are
migratory and the forgotten shows through as correction.
This noun has been defunct for centuries.
May I have it, just this once, this while
upon which the wind is so insistent?
Collage has made a chaos of my desk.
But the interior strain is intolerable
when character is evoked: under the ashtray,
a young girl's eyes looking out from her image.
Was she brave? Have I told you about my uncle,
my cousin, my mother seeing a tall man on some steps
and deciding there and then on my life?
In your dream, you were flayed
by the inflection of recovered speech, the earlier
moment in a dark car with an old friend driving.
Things we don't do take up residence as facts
and, as facts, we desire them. I wonder how my garden is.

*to Chet Wiener*

# LAKEVIEW DINER

A chair, half-hidden behind leaves;
a torso, emerging from pigment;
a girl, on the outskirts;
this is how all my beginnings are.
I fell asleep reading a book.
Was the brief dream astute?
We know memory is crooked, is interlude,
but natural elision is part of our booty,
and is why I cannot know myself
better than you do, and you know me
better than I. I resemble the girl
in the paragraph. So here we are,
each of us, in the abrasive gleam
of our settings, hunched over sections
of the newspaper. We greet each other
with the unobtrusive fanfare of a waitress:
*Howdy folks, what'll it be today?*
Her hand on a rag. Her hand on the rag
steers from edge to edge, like a wind
over the lake. *I'd like*
*the late afternoon reflected in the lake*
*and that upturned leaf which appears to be a duck.*
*Hold the light.* This is how all my middles are.
Now we can relax against the speaking other
like the adjacent dawn leaning on its day,
furthering. But what? The trap and scandal
we voted for yesterday, but did not choose.
*Know ye what ye want,* said the wise man,
*but be sure ye knoweth the consequences*
*of what ye want.* So now we embark
on the chill voyage out into the numbered
scheme of things.
And the days swarm up and away
into the agility of brief reverence;
the duck returns to a leaf.
Call these actions ourselves delayed.
We are kept by the indefinite, aroused.

*to Jack*

# NOT THAT IT COULD BE FINISHED

She holds a conversation with her ornaments,
stray or contingent, heaped in patches
darkly and then loosened
onto the table to be consumed.
Collect me, they seem to ask,
into an assembly; construe us
like any morning onto any day.
Bring us forward notch by notch
into a paradigm of comfort
to be clasped: any cup will do.
Any dance? Take a seed
and blow it toward the curtain
which, like a bright shield
hugging breasts into radiance,
is seen and spoken of and desired.
Will any silence fit? So many
columns of air are held upright
in inebriated passage,
so many paper stacks
brittle under the weight
of what was news to attentive readers
as zones of holy strangers
feed through tunnels their imported cares.
Stare at us, they seem to say,
we are windows propped up against the sky,
quotations of light waiting to sail
into your aperture, calling *because because*
and *now now now.* And the good body
is pulled over the original rapacious body
like a huge sock, its cornucopia
of sour wind and dust emptied into the firmament.

# ANNOTATION

Even accidents falter. The room behind the room
has lost its particularity, a tent
in a field of tents.
These are like the endings of words
as rooms resemble the beginnings.
Will she choose? As between metal and cloth,
duration over flexibility, easy handling, touch?
She lay in the brown October grass under an imported sky.
Or, standing inside, she gazes out at the real thing
shifting behind glass.
To say sky in the face of sky
is a failure of duration;
the sky escapes.
                    The suburbs are plain,
especially in winter, if to be plain
is to be similar. But this
harbors difference in its midst.
Eventually it will become
the fabulous plaintiff absurdly jeweled,
a city ready to explore
all the oblique ruins of the unsaid.
The unhealed voices soar
into the predawn like accelerating notes
in a choral mood. All night, she
hears them, and turns away, and hears again
the refrain of the unspeakable rhyme
and wakes to first light spelling its shield.

# AFTER THE STORM

What the afternoon assumes is
that we will live through it, as well as in it.
But what if, in thunder, in high wet wind,
it tore from us, left us here
unframed in the raw conduit, marginal
and scared? Were it truly haphazard
it would be like that
but we must trust, we must be game.

I will tell you about the soprano
and I will tell you about the cool air's form.
Writing now, I think of her,
of how she smiles into the capitulated yes
of her ruined kindness, her voice
swaddled in archives of her self.
She sings into the butterfly weed and fog
only it is not a song, it is

her desire to sing and her desire not to sing.
The wet, heavy fog rolls in
and the weed is burning at the edge of the meadow.
Her trouble is the trouble of fiction and dolls;
she is authored by another, one who says
*Sing! Do not sing!* and does not watch
as the weed fires along the meadow
and does not see the fog roll over her toward us.

# REPORT

Too much drudgery binds the tongue.
The obdurate loosens its hold,
a nonchalant mask foiling
a reward as of a natural sling
garlanded, sleepless, fervent.
It had asked us to come away
and to touch everything we passed
down the staircase hollow,
under the blue rocks,
into the broken bodies distributed
where alms could not reach,
between the curtains and the glass,
on the stinking sheets,
into the smoke-scented air's pulleys,
the inexhaustible list of lists
and its absurd author's abject test.
Why did I come inside to tell you this?
Did someone call? Do I remember being called?
To wash, yes, to eat, yes, to sleep
but not to step over the shape
curled in the hall, its body's huge loop
hung in the mind like a shadow
that must be surpassed. Had I been asked
to tidy the forest floor, *pick it up, pick it up,*
dead boughs, tiny gray leaves, stone upon stone,
dust, wings, moss, and fill up the holes
of each sarcophagus leeching icy water,
mend the ripped ferns, untie the knots
of each web and nest. Had I said
no I will follow this trail, these subjects
until they are depleted
because all the women and girls came in.

# TOCK

A night without edition, virtual:
a hearing. Yes, and yes its sleeve
gapes to house the air's thin shine.
An old path is traced
obscurely along the meridian
near to where our ancient kin were
and were buried in loam, preserving them.
A smooth crest, a young boy's brow.
I walked with him one afternoon in winter
as the ferns shook under the dazzling rise.

Under the dazzling rise the ferns shake
verdigris on copper. This day
we go to the field where a battle was lost.
We see them toppled on the plain
like ropes frayed, untwisted.
He says, *I am going to kiss you here.*
We meet barefoot girls
weeping, their footsteps in damp, torn grass.
In damp grass, tearing air, the girls weep.

The women are sad, and old.
They picket the house.
Now the girls are in a barn
where they will be photographed by men
who smell of oil and straw and brandy.
The walls are hung with useful tools, straps.
Later, the barn is a staircase
hung with pictures of children smiling.
They are on a ladder. The roofline extends.
The roofline is an arm extending the night.

*From*

# BEFORE RECOLLECTION
### (1987)

# SUBJECT TO CHANGE

Those of us who are there will never leave.
Given our inability to make a version,
one that does not twist
off the ground, the same ground we have
imagined, separately,
the thing casts itself into being.
Such impediments cannot be altered.
Other ideas are lost.
Are they ideas? What thing?
Once there was possibility
but now that too is gone
predicting the river.
Is it all, and will it stay
longer than usual,
gathering hesitancy only because it
is new, until, heavily absorbent,
boundaries fail, as if of ash?
The sky was something else, massive
but kind, leaving nothing in its wake.
Often I have thought the linear
duplicitous, mapping outer and inner,
showing us core and enclosure
as it helps itself over destiny's rail.
The difference is the air's lunar kiss,
a residual, if despondent, bearing.
Those of us who leave were never there.

*to Thomas Nozkowski*

# THE VANQUISHED

A deeper sun
saying this mirth, this imperfect grappling
with underpinnings.
Toothless, smiling: a rind.
Or, organized never again to predict,
the most sequestered is
aroused, and so shown to be explicit
after all. Summoned from the inequalities
of daring, ourselves, exampling,
manage to find our way to the well
where unsafe foothills
and insurmountable calligraphies
rinse upward.
                    We search for apt signatures
where they aren't, the names
bathed out of reach
as when invention immerses fact.
I mean the way she hurried to meet him
and was almost too late, as
I hurry and am too late
because here it is
falling across without benediction
or wanly imagined, as in these jars
lovely with dry things. After a while
the seasons, turning, twitch,
no longer sedated, nor expectant,
uneasily seeded.

*to Bill Jensen*

# POEM FOR MARGRIT, FOR FRIDA

The elusive recitation—
blacks submerged in cold suds
relaxed from shape, less
hope or help than,
dry, in heaps, on the black floor,
at the very least wearable—
the recitation abridged
so that panic and ardor
are picked from a general sense
of something depicted, some chord
struck: the soldier's collar up
against cold, or her heart
submerged in the ruddy glow of paint
and weaponry or weeds piercing the shoulders
where we expect to find neither flesh nor air.
In another ethos, wings would prevail.

In rare instances, the iconic
is translated precisely:
vocal, serene, if layered.
I write this way for mystery and need,
the images endeavoring to fold
around a central nerve,
and to salvage what is worn from wear.

*to Margrit Lewczuk*

# CLOSING HOURS

This trace, if it exists, is alms for delusion.
An arch uncurls from the floor
scented with the scent of a tapestry, housed here.
I recall the hour but not its passage
unless dream captures and ties it to sleep:
a fat bellhop smiles, shows me to the tower
where I can watch the departure.
But some days settle so that nothing
crosses the horizon; stare as I will, no star
needles the air. Now I am left
on the outskirts of a forest hemmed in by wheat
where plump trees hide the image, its symmetry
shot up and blown across the ground like feathers.
The unicorn, the grail, blue and red wings
of kneeling musicians, these are embroidered
elsewhere. Perseverance was crowned.
Hope and Pity prayed for success.
How fast is this camera? Can it record a trace?
There was a voyage. Four mounted horses
strain against centuries.
To each is allotted: dust kicked up, smoke, plumage.

# PSYCHE'S DREAM

If dreams could dream, beyond the canon of landscapes
already saved from decorum, including mute
illicit girls cowering under eaves
where the books are stacked and which they
pillage, hoping to find not events but response

If dreams could dream, free from the damp crypt
and from the bridge where she went
to watch the spill and the tree
standing on its head, huge and rootless
(Of which the wasp is a cruel illustration

although its sting is not), the decay
now spread into the gardens, their beds
tethered to weeds and to all other intrusions;
then the perishing house, lost from view
so she must, and you, look out to see
not it but an image of it, would be

nowhere and would not resemble, but would languish
on the other side of place where the winged boy
touches her ear far from anywhere
but gathered like evening around her waist
so that within each dream is another, remote
and mocking and a version of his mouth on her mouth.

# STILL

The sleeping urgencies are perhaps ruined now
in the soul's haphazard sanctuary,
ignored like a household
dormant in the landscape, a backwoods dump
where the last care has worn through its last
memory. We might think of this as a blessing
as we thrash in the nocturnal waste:
rubble of doors, fat layers of fiber
drooping under eaves, weeds
leaning in lassitude after heavy rain
has surged from a whitened sky.
Thunder blooms unevenly in unknowable places
breaking distance into startling new chambers
we cannot enter; potentially, a revelation.

*Deep Midnight,* a song on the Chinese zither.
This must be long after the storm, long
after the revolution. It seems some things
were kept in storage after all: cool air
quietly throbbing, a few candles, chance songs
*Soul to Soul* on the radio. Chance is a variant
of change, the weather changing, chancy
but destined. Our trust is that we, too, are
forms attached to content, content to meanings
aroused. It is our custom to bring things about.

# SAINT LUCIA

1.

Suppose it is enough: rock, tree, sky,
these uncounted, unaccountable surfaces.
And suppose this is the entrance
among these hills
that sound high, far-off, look old,
hooded, sloped, ending with an owl, a cup.
Through lime-slit leaves
light travels, a rag.
There are tangles everywhere, and salt.
Under the leg of a chair, its rim half-shining.
The sea in the distance, its rim half-shining.

2.

Not quite fledged the surfaces change
more-or-less dangerous, as if
partly digested or not yet evolved.
Tuesday; o'clock.
Direction is peripheral,
a shapeless vicinity cast by net.
Light is a rag. Leaf, bird, that.
Silence, rescinded as wings,
marries air to yellowness.
There are dictions here
that adhere to necessity, to speech not said.

3.

Between the ominous and transcendent sea,
each present as light determines,
are insignias: triangles at large, passings.
Everything is wordless but palpable.
The harbor with its vessels.
The sky with its slow baggage.
The mind with its vessels, its baggage.
Clouds come from the same direction
slowly over the hills, encumbered passengers.

There is nothing between us
but the play of these various casual leaves.

4.

The sea, solitary or not,
implies the confines of a dream.
I'm between Beckett and Bishop,
the one entirely in, the other there
civilizing Brazil, clarity to clarity.
I'd rather be a fishwife or a frog.
a secretary taking dictation.
*Do this. Do that.*
Respite from the brave and intent.
The mango I ate under that flat-leaved tree
tastes better than any imagined thing,
salt erased by sweet
intoxicating, solitary, a tongue within.

5.

Dipping back to gather some quality,
not the stone but the color of the stone
as it travels, light's motif,
to land on the rim of a cup.
The words might be seen
lying here on the beach
complete and distinct in sameness.
And I have kept you with me
as a version of nearness
to say what I am kept from saying
here, on the beach, with stones piled up.

6.

The drone flies up to take a queen.
He dies ecstatic, founding an empire.
Such an aspiration! Such requital!
When things get crowded she leaves,
takes up home in a cave
with a swarm of workers and eunuch drones.
The hummingbird has been each day

to stick its long thing into the blooms.
Conrad says, *"The mere incidents of the surface,*
*the reality, the reality I tell you fades."*
Light is delayed on the opaque leaves.

7.

Or suppose not.
A cup is not an inlet.
The hours climb up the hunch-backed hills.
Thursday; o'clock.
The owl has its habits.
Everything seems random, diffuse,
as images collect
into some quality, as of surfaces intact.
The lizard visits twilight
down one leg of a chair, across the porch.
The hills end with passage, a cup, a call.

8.

They clamor to get out: rat, rag, owl,
the hummingbird, its radiant stick,
and the three-note call.
The hens are parading and dull.
Leaves keep moving; they want to be winged.
The syntax of solitude is
to witness versions that clock and petal,
enfolding instances. Among these hills
that are high, far-off, hooded, old,
sloped, ending with a cup.
The thing is handed to us. We hand it back.
In the diction of surfaces, a distinguished absence.

# HOLDING AIR

The day's accuracies, however feeble, are not
domestic although the line they draw
is encumbered, possibly even daunted
by that smudge I know is a river.
And now you know it as it slides
onto the sky, an unguent soothing the horizon.
You care also to know who you are.
Nothing so much as view but more than noise,
for the hum pertains to you, fanning the interior
and entering here through the window's screen.
I had forgotten this attenuated lapse
between us, a sort of moat spun around us
as we collapse from day to day,
each of us ammunition for the other and
for the night. The rope on the low roof
is strung like a hammock holding air,
doubling back on itself, limp,
catching a glimpse of sun better than the water.
Here it comes again, the light
reined in, riding that rope from wall to wall.

# AS FAR AS THE EYE CAN SEE

Perhaps the weather has nothing to say
other than the simple duress of cause and effect
we muster into forbearance,
so little of which is left it takes on desire
as when reticence reaches its limit,
signals an embrace. The wind is favorable
even as it thrashes the stipulating tree
into panic, an urgency beyond its means,
reminding us of how much better it would be
to know less and therefore not impart meaning
to things left well enough alone.
This the weather never does
and is why all the turbulent paintings
only suggest the carriage of light
mattering everywhere, or the rain, stricken,
conversing with familiar distances of earth.
And now I wonder if intimacy is tonal,
some agreement of parts along the surface
weather, refusing to rest, narrates
with all the clarity words might articulate to us.

# MONODY

This utterance is not jazz,
inspired by digression but loyal to fate,
arriving back on time to meet up with song.
Left to its own devices, the soul is furtive,
scavenging thrift to make ends meet:
plays with Psyche's hair, pokes at the air
where music is, talks to itself
as it waits for public transportation
to take it through a windy reverie or street.
Colloquies occur, bunched on the curb
like marigolds no one picks
or names that come to mind unattended.
It takes a route around revelation
knowing you are in the next room
where the screening is, where the scene shifts
fatally as on the tip of my tongue
or a dream that plummets into morning.
Last night we rode a pinwheel across the sea.
We kissed goodbye again and I think last words
were said as I passed you the umbrella:
it was about to rain; I was about to wake up.
What happens gains momentum
but these forms are murderous in intent:
contrived by oblivion, curtailed by release,
and now the narrative sky is sprayed with birds in flight.

# NAMING THE HOUSE

The ample, plain snow inhibits detail
but frees splendor briefly, completely,
like a dream ornamented with a consoling retrieval:
balsam gathered at the top of the stairs
at the Chappaqua house. And I think
of how we might walk out onto the pond
unknowingly, cross the slight curb
onto ice, trusting similitude's throw of white.
And I think also of how women, toward evening,
watch as the buoyant dim slowly depletes
terrain, and frees the illuminated house
so we begin to move about, reaching for potholders
and lids, while all the while noting
that the metaphor of the house is ours to keep
and the dark exterior only another room
waiting for its literature.
She dallies now in plots
but feels a longing for dispersal,
for things all to succumb to the night's snow
omitting and omitting. She has this attention:
to the reticent world enforced by the sensual
and her curiosity, a form of anticipation,
knowing the failure of things to null and knowing, too,
the joy of naming it this, and this is mine.

# LANDSCAPE WITH VASE

Predatory, then, or rushed,
self breaks into categories of self:
here flies away, here waits, here resembles
ancient tenacities of fruit
and of the sorrow of petals:

collapsed, partial, redolent, wet.
And I could say such moments contract
when it enters another phase
and is consumed, as the bloom
opens to full stature and brands emptiness

crowding it out.
Now it diminishes like a remote era
seemingly irrelevant, not knowing
the faith of disciples,
how they wept when it faltered

and went about barefoot, unseemly, detached.
Definition pares down. A slow cloud
lifts light off the grass and slides it
downhill to where the roses are.
Things take on the look of potential:

a mild shadow is sometimes consoling
and might lead to stillness, simple containment.

# CAROUSEL

To embark it lifts, flies up, scans the view:
the river, slit between highway and sky;
the sky, a distant plinth
set between deckle-edged bricks.
She likes the way it comes out of the blue.
Inside, petals are temporarily blazed,
light as Japanese sleeves in the wind.
Those were purple, dye of purple herbs
brushed on silk, unpluckable, walking across.
*"Won't the guards see you wave your sleeves to me?"*

Nevertheless she is afraid.
She does not know how to cross paths and stop.
Images keep her awake, waiting.
What comes out of the blue? Why smile?
There it flies low over inclined fields,
a dossier of wings. Elsewhere,
an outline on a box indicating prowess.
She gets the binoculars out to see up close.
Copper pans are dusty on the wall
and she is full of tears, the dread of tears.

Above the river: an outline of smokestacks.
They could be set to music or dance,
but she is waiting for the mist to rise.
Her wish? Carnal, flamboyant. A landscape
charged, noisy, dangerous,
faintly dangerous as she crosses the street.
She knows things spread, shadow enlarging image,
illicit perceptions of blue, gentian evenings.
Altering goes on, even on days that are mostly night,
and she is rapt, watching, almost heraldic.

I like masks, deeper shades of blue,
how it concludes black.
A swimmer is adorned with one arm
rising out of the blue.

A man in the sea.
A painting of a man in the sea.
I like the way it comes out of the blue.
The horse rises and falls; my sleeves are waving.
It is not dark that scares me, but the limit
which places the house in the field, the horse in its stall.

A bald supple surface falls between cracks
as the door slowly opens.
Light is one way to wake up, image another,
but she must tiptoe across the floor
to tell her secret. The floor is cold.
She does not know how to say it.
We must invent a new mood,
gargoyles, scents, purple-robed figures
walking the courtyard.
The horse did not fly up. The horse is wingless.

Those who never loved him say
he was witness to dust, shelter of his hours,
among the faithless, faithless.
They cannot see in the dark.
We are gregarious, blind dolls.
Over her shoulder, the painting depicts will.
Staring at the view, she has a sense of place
and of omission. The ways in which we live
are earmarked for letting go, and so
she makes her descent, plucks it, rises into the blue.

# BEFORE RECOLLECTION

Here we begin: not to let purposes transcend making.
All day in the shadow of, and then
to propose a critical approach to, love
or color or the vindictive aspects of spring.
Descent is optional, even as we twine
in the vicinity of grace,
an aspect of mourning, hoping to find
someone to help the heart without question.

There is another morning when we twine
in the center of grace, helpless,
and find emblems for now
and dream somewhat.
What is yours is mine, stacked
against the season as allowance without thrift
so the requiem lifts hours to the sky,
dilutes rose, then dries into night.
You say there is some place like never
but these trees resemble a former green
held in abeyance, branched, becoming inordinate.

*to Brian Conley*

# MEDIEVAL EVENING

Earliness treads, curtailing momentum
but cool and lavish as wind:
torpor vanished, myth reawakened.
As if surprise still lurked
sucking at daylight, fundamental
to windows: trumpets, guardian saints,
a host of angels visible for once as fact
even as we confuse murder with genius
and fulfill ourselves with the unfulfilled.
I grant you this face, these arms, this respite,
a merry-go-round spinning into night, ardent.
I grant you this battalion of blues
to ease you so that you might
forgive the twilight its faint praise
of an innate beauty, missed and retrieved daily.

# LAKE OF ISLES

Dimly perceived coast
caressed where water is
where lucid stretches finger belief
on occasion and the aftermath of occasion.
Seen from here, night is measured,
and stories no longer hold permanence.
Days adhere and a faint wind
anoints our giving with something
limitless: eddies pull and turn
set loose in reaches where no harbor is.

If only I could regard the perpetual
as calm and slaked, not couched
in the unforeseen or
tied into remnants
as if, having touched you once
I had touched you always
and could stay in the bonds of this lake
as part of a readiness: awakened, awake.

# TOPAZ

Some treason we have come to know as
belonging to pleasure, the way city streets
invite deliverance, and all
the in-betweens we have come, also, to know.
Having, not having, slips between windows
where plastic calf and sequined brow move,
late on, to desire. Gradually, I admit
to wanting you, as if you
were real, not just an arrangement with time.
Within each of us the autonomous declares,
enters barefoot, turns off the lights, gives itself up.

# PATH

                              What is
is that you might declare
characteristically,
by an assumed nearness or slope
whose reason to be eager is also
the reticence you shield from entirety.
Under which I find myself cast.
Is this something like mercy,
the better solitude, when
attaching herself to the morning's press
she makes for herself a habit
from the simplest stuff, testing this
agenda only? And if not, why not?
The occasion is meant to be witnessed.
Blade after blade, the curve delves.

In this way urgency wells,
nicknamed history, but in fact
a slow banquet taking place down by the sea
or lake or, since it is essential,
any place that tells of itself evenings.
It is in my interest to follow
although you are nowhere
to be seen. You know where.

# COASTAL

This sort of thing happens.
The implausible converts under pressure
the pressure of night carriers
who begin to sing
in flat territories of the central region.
I suppose all awakenings serve to refresh
even when the place is untraveled or
afternoon after afternoon
depleted uniquely.
But some mornings usurp
sleepless meanwhiles
when conjuring begins
far under the tower of lights.
And so goes elsewhere, climbs
the steep coast road above the village
giddy and starkly obedient. Below,
the Adriatic is the same as the beautiful
and the will comes back to make it
out of the thing stressed almost into being.
Or look away, *into* the rock.

# APERTURE

It does not come as hairline fractures
mapping plaster with brittle rivers
nor with the unmeasured gait
of a tulip's averting grace
(lathed to half-rhyme with death)
while these others, these anemones,
peel back Giotto's choir of angels
plummeting and stayed, frescoes of disbelief
that came only by faith, never by description
which cannot save despite its comforts
as we might say: *touch me here,*
*put your hand here where it hurts.* Where
is it? What is the unimaginable source of it?
This transparent stain left on the air where was is.

# VERNAL ELEGY

Crammed into a corner, the heart
does no good to swell
into another image: the sea
listing too easily; hard buds
breathing into their mute precocity
even as we give our best love freely
over the counter, an announcement
in the here and now.
                          Wind
might leave a legacy also,
slants and shreds as well as deeper abrasions
on the face, and the dunes ride high
and the cliffs stay. Ping!
The smallest sphere collides, dispersing
there surely to change what is recoverable.
Those who are told can't tell.
Only those who knew now know.

*In memory: Constance Ernst Bessie*

# A SIMPLE SERVICE

And now the day
comes slowly on us, perfumed, cool,
wherein amnesty and tide
are part of what we thought was passing
but which is headed our way, bearing down,
about to seal us off
while the rest strut from cartoon to cartoon
mouthing wisecracks and *phooey*
as the ditch, that place where things occur,
fills to the rim with brine
and with the last peonies of the season.

The gentle guise that summer is
is our right to pass, and for our sake
we have taken our cues from the garden,
standing under the canopy with allegiance
to the calm voice speaking for us, blessing ash.
Always I had wanted to speak calmly
like a landscape just after rain
when radiance is styled for perception
the day the last ancient is placed
beside father, mother and sister
on a green afternoon overlooking life.
Those who remain are implied, being here now.

# THE WALLED PALACE

In the hierarchy of the day we are made agile,
persuade ourselves to play-down generation,
pause in mapping out. They met
under a table in Mexico. The drums beat wildly
as long-legged birds—those ashtray birds—
strutted, raved. The flea market
has these things for sale, so next day
only fragments are reclaimed.
*"My husband is my drummer and my band leader."*

Sometimes to say is to have
so we can pass from the room empty-handed.
Concurrently, there are things to see:
a band of windows and, beyond,
tall comical trees that winter green.
At best things are untidy, latent, fugitive.
Words fail where no present is
and we age in our own narration.
We are, Pascal said, so unwise
as to wander in times to which we don't belong,
choose *seraglio* over other possibilities, other homes.

# NARROW MARGINS

We have leafed through these margins enough to know
they are not vacations, but absence readied
not unlike a young girl on her way to bed
in a strange place, a narrow sky
hung with cares and lies on unseen ropes
and held by a system of passions.
Here all is renovated, enclosed.
What once passed as dream
(those candid dragons, fed on Ajax,
who flew nightly beyond the curve of fate)
turns one day into a wrought-iron gate
strapped with fat red bouquets and unsigned notes.

Death is not simple; it starts a process.
Later, she moves to L.A. He flies south.
She phones for zip codes and news.
Just before dinner he excused himself, went
somewhat unwell to bed where he grew cold
and awkward, too awkward to be asleep.
The morgue is closed for the holidays.
There are cards, four deep, across the mantelpiece.
The poet gives a performance in which he is an owl.
The photographer gives a talk on how long color lasts.
The year ends. We are forced to the place of amazement.

# LATER THAT EVENING

Wood laid in for the winter; the rest of the century.
*"I used to know everything about fish,"*
he claimed, staring at the flame
on the mast of the gondola,
its miniature gold hull afloat on the table.
*"Skate fish, blows, sea thrush*
*and rare heart of bass*
*we used to fish at the Vineyard, summers."*
A silent film called *Snow* is shown at the window.
*"This is bliss for me,"* she offered,
*"this absence."* Outside, something exhaled
and the surprised birds sang to it.
Midnight dawn; eternal preamble.
And the real world? There, where the estate
of the imagined ends: trees cut up, fishbones left.

From

# MANY TIMES, BUT THEN

## (1979)

*Ought not these oldest sufferings of ours to be yielding*
*more fruit by now? Is it not time that, in loving,*
*we freed ourselves from the loved one, and, quivering, endured:*
*as the arrow endures the string, to become, in the gathering out-leap,*
*something more than itself? For staying is nowhere.*

—RAINER MARIA RILKE, *"First Elegy"*

# A VISIT TO THE COUNTRY

There are legends which please the inner ear,
that part that yearns, does not hear
but knows when the mechanical rabbit is slain
by the real thing. The real thing
revokes the vulgar indiscriminate corpse
into pain of birth, told and retold
by the woman who otherwise does not speak.

She stops drinking and digs holes for roses.
One is called Chicago Peace, bred
to resemble the white rose on the tapestry
in which the unicorn distills myth from history.
She thinks of Saint Francis as the bluebirds nest
in a small wood box. They exist, but
Saint Francis is a reverie among bald, silent monks.
On an island in the pond two turtles shine.
They wait centuries for the geese to lay.

# GRAMERCY PARK EVENING

I am, in these instances, aware
there is much to be desired, much left to desire,
and the rest abided. The late hour has everything
turned down; even the constant fleet of wheels
is another noise: less. I was trying to sleep
and to imagine us near the sea, the light
skinny and unhedged, the sea
a ribbed plate, a wide blue absolute
into which pink is introduced like an idea in music.

Desire is an aspect of ethics; belief is not.
You can move a peach across the table
without changing its color but the light, this light,
casts a shadow of doubt. What we perceive
is part dream, part deceit; what we want
touches knowledge. The park is something you
could not know about: late afternoon, a walk,
the walk I sometimes took towards a cadence
of real images: the gate, the grass, the lock.
There was a sense that things are lit
from within, of high, shut carriages and women in hats.

# THEN SUDDENLY

The bloom, stranded somehow in glass and a view
of marvelous, slow-moving things
nameless because I had run out of names.
Measures had to be taken.
But I had been to New Jersey and back
and hadn't even noticed the bridge.
Talk is a way of not looking.
But notice how he sits in his chair
without so much as a color on his mind
while at the same time light
accrues behind a mass of leaves. Now
everything is darker. I think she is on a cruise
in the Black Sea wearing her portrait
(how we see her, dream of her)
while at the same time worried about the farm.
She told me what comes to mind is
*then suddenly,* an icon
for which she is never prepared but always knows.
I was trying to get at it, the way
it goes awkwardly forward on the pavement
until it takes hold, draws
out of the drive across the bridge
lights strung ahead in litanies of sudden knowledge.

# ALONG THE WAY

What caused a musical persuasion and what
gained entrance was at first
limited: an alteration in the span
of the gradual. We could not yet fix a name.
And in not fixing a name, we went ahead
with a sense of pages turning
and of music getting lost on arrival.
The rain, lasting, helped
as if it were a mention, a sign of its effect
allowed by what we knew all during:
that it would also not rain and we would know it.
We were on an excursion,
that was clear, but
we did not dare to take anything along
even though we stopped from time to time
to make a presentation: *"I give you this."*
This was something we had given before
and therefore had an emptiness
or a pause in substance but we could not do
otherwise, given the extent
of what had gone before: the formal part.
The inclusions were drenched but discrete.
We had learned to hear it note by note
and to arrive, perilous but glad, at the disclosed.

# WINTER SKY

Add to what you already know
the fact that it is severely cold today
and add that to the difficulty of the literal
because the literal somehow misses
the way you can miss
the blue sky on a cold day.

But because it turns out
that life is essentially an old string
on which we bead beads, some of which match,
we cannot help but mention the same thing
over and over, as the sky mentions blue.

As for you, you
have probably taken it lightly, you
are so good at doling out events
that cause recollection, like that day
you pulled something across the future
and the sky was blue.

# TRUE AND FALSE GREEN

All these balloons hovering. No wind.
First thing in the morning when
this repeats that, not yet
invaded by frozen foods although
the peas are intensely green
just like the balloons.
                    And the one lost marble
is also green, its dusty circumference
stuck far under the radiator
remote as architecture.
                        Unseasonably mild.
Now Bette Davis struts out
a wounded witch or a lame mechanical bird
angular with contempt. My hip blocks the view.
I hear you hate words because they color the truth.

# THE WHITE SEQUENCE

1.

Now it moves towards declaration, I try
to embody the future
by changing my clothes over and over.
Finally: an old pink T-shirt
under the black Moroccan blouse,
elaborately stitched,
I bought for an occasion. And
I have changed my rings from silver
to gold.
        There are distractions:
the smell of toast up through floors
and the bunch of orange flowers
that will live to bridge the seasons.
The first snow is snowing in the Midwest.

2.

One could always go to the Hebrides, or Kansas.
Anywhere where there is profuse
nothing, nothing but air in motion
and distances to boggle the imagination.
Or one could stay at home and count
all the white things as if searching
for the exception to a rule. A rule of thumb.
A rule of eye. A rule of heart. What
rules the heart?
        Dr. Johnson toured the Hebrides.
Of Sunday he said, *"It should be different
from another day. People may walk, but not
throw stones at birds. There may be
relaxation, but there should be no levity."*

3.

What is it about? Skirting the issue
and such costumes as we found in the attic.
You know mother wore these

delicate dresses and you know how long ago
everything gets. Her mother
looked out the window and said
it was all yellow. It was all rose, but
white at the edge.
            At the edge, I stare
to keep from slipping, but it's clear
I cannot oppose this inwardness.
My great-aunt was a painter. She
made delicate paintings of woodland scenes.
She is extremely old now and bites her nurse.

4.

Nothing speaks for itself. Why is this box
full of unwrapped gifts? The frog
has turquoise eyes and the bracelet is made
from carved ivory. Here is a hand
in the form of an ashtray. Someone
is saving up for something unexpected.

A rainy day? No, today is cold
and the sun is making forays onto brick.
The two white candles have never been lit
and the ivy is almost dancing
from thirst. One day
we walked far into the woods
and saw a dead tree which curved and curved.

5.

You wonder all the time
how you got here and invent
another life, past or future, by which
to come back. The dry things help.
Everything is essentially frail and brown.
The leaves are braille on the ground
and the sky is coming into permanent white.

Most of the people you know are almost mad.
You are mad and talk to yourself

as if you existed, wearing make-up
familiar as winter but always smiling.
The next time you will return as a clown
and speak only with gestures of gloved hands.

6.

How about simple exhaustion, like a crease?
After a while you run out of examples
and have to change course.
I think this is my last example.
Now I am free to roam, free
to join the singers on the road to Buffalo.
Tomorrow I will hire a van
and have it painted white
and wire it for sound
and line it with satin
and head out. I will invite no one.
It will be the first example of something else.
There is a rudimentary addition in life
and there is the need to subtract, or erase.

7.

I would not have waited gladly longer.
Today's design is clarity and height,
almost free of history. One night
we were almost free of history.
Each thing has that white on white
the way these bricks, hit by sun,
stop passage but still define it.

The flowers in the blue vase have died
but the leaves of the big plant
hold up luminosities, which change.
And tonight, the placemats imply
a literal possibility. As you come
to tell me what it is you are going
to tell me, I eye things for transience.

# CONFIGURATION OF ONE

A friend wrote: *"you know of course
the 'you' in that short piece I wrote
beginning 'I dreamed that you were in
my dream' etc. was you"* and you know
last night I dreamed
someone had put a fine wire
across my path and I tripped.
And I told someone the reason I thought
I like green so much is because
I was once a bird. *"An owl,"* he said.
Some people have said I was
in Italy during the time of the Medici
but I think it was earlier, back
when Giotto was pressing angels into
flat chapel walls. When you came
into the room last night I was that again.

# GRAY MORNING

There are oils that slip us out of place
and we are too far away to believe in anything, much less
the nearness of the singular. You, asleep, aside,
crouch by a river watching slivers collide.
The heat is unbearable, the air
carries nothing back from the coast except birds
which are always present like a vivid, extreme desire.
Did you ever climb the mountain? I stare
where we were, where there is nothing to look for.

Meanwhile, cups are loose in grades of gray.
Decisions must be made between pearl and mercury,
shades of meaning only painters know, as only painters
see ingredients. How will green yield to pearl
or yellow hang on mercury? There is always color
where the body lay; not the dream, but its impact.
The names of things accost us as we wake.

Where are you? I don't care. I care
how you look as you get up to go, in search of the thing
you think you miss. What you see in the distance
never gets close, the allure
of slender reeds and girls, of blue jackets and pearls,
an inventory of images by which we make ourselves real.
You move from the water, altogether far.
Light ventures the window and touches down, profusely near.

# POEM

If only it were a matter of wet strawberries
among wet lettuces, or the mauve gray haze
on the road north. The decors
rush in and we are sated by looking
but there are other colorations, other codes.
There were frogs all over the airport.
There was nothing around but France.
And there are the nights when a long caress
breaks through the film of sleep
yielding something unspeakably true.

I wanted to say: *all I want inside is you.*
I did not, because you are not
all that I want. If I insist, and I do,
on always including you, it is because
I foresee no other anchor when things are
so windy and culpable. We must return to the day
we were shattered into care, even
with the severe things going on in front of us.

# ROMANCE

She said nothing; he mentioned his daughter.
They met, one evening, in a room without coercion
and from there digressed to a place
remote as a park and as wandering: grass
littered with small defects, fountains waterless.
They forgot their hobbies and skipped out on
real appointments with friends. Hair, mouth, skin.
They knew them, perched on a limb each morning, singing.

He despised summer, the risky season, melodious,
thick air entangled air netting journeys he dreamed of;
choice itself a violence. He craved
an immune but legible haven where he might raise himself
to Kingdom Come. He lay in bed, her face
overhead, obliterating: a Byzantine portrait.
He mentioned his daughter: *"Everyone starts with image,
clutching the long white doll that precedes illusion."*

She said nothing, searched the attic for clues.
The old pictures stabbed, vindictive, private:
someone standing by a fence in front of a garden.
She came across letters irrevocably folded
and dreamed they were a shape tangible in space, of
huge porcelains cast at her feet by an entirely white man.
She sent a grave wind to molest him; he vanished.
Each moment jettisoned desire until they were wicked with loss.

*to Emile Fallaux*

# AS IT TURNS OUT

Desdemona, whose name comes to mind
like the taste of pineapple, steps through
the door in her torn skirt and looks up.
*"Still raining."* As it turns out
this is a slipshod universe, not
the opulent crystal chandelier
she ordered from Tiffany for the diningroom.
Bricks fall down the shaft
of things in general, to turn up
a day later in a book of photographs.
Her heart is permanently overcast.
She will need to wear a coat until a new age
dawns, its light filtered like charm
through a crowded, uncomfortable room.
She'll move on. A marriage will take place
although by then her looks will have changed
as well as her character. She'll slide
down the banister, all smiles, all dressed up.

# THE DAY AFTER

An island is not a window onto a broad climate
but a caption describing what is beyond
and illegible. The tides are high,
the light rivets and we are aware
of an intrinsic mode less probable than music.
The sound is the pitch of a shell, a brilliance
that parades before us as if we were marooned
in some incessant necessary garden
or an ancient resort furnished with intimacies.
By now the moon does not count as the moon
slips out of sight into the abstract, the luminous.

There are no vertical landscapes, just
a low, monotonous museum lit from within by
other, giant lights. The windows are shuttered.
By the time we arrive it is too late
and we know why some houses seem blind and others
merely logical. We cannot intrude on these limits;
even the dunes are the occasion of dull enterprise.
The fires, for instance. How many are deliberately set?
Last winter's snow was sobering: she walked across
in a purple coat and the birds were held down, pecking.

*in memory: Matthew Carlebach*

# LAST NIGHT IT RAINED

There never was a gate, although is seemed possible
to walk through to where the farm may have been.
A platter of flowers had been brought in
and I had continued to sleep
enclosed by rain fencing the distance.
The animals had all been painted into the landscape
and everyone was tired of invention; tired, even,
of the sort of thing that stares you in the face
dull with hunger.
                   Halfway across the field we stopped.
There was no way to be admitted, despite
the fact that we would be known on sight.
What lie would I tell? Sometimes the provocation
made me giddy, and I flirted around the periphery
just outside the frame where air gets at the edges,
raking oblivion. I woke up aware
that the whole night had been spent
in trivial but terrifying proximities: someone had said
*wipe your nose* and someone else had hated the plates.
The month had changed overnight: now
the season would not let go, the air stubborn and clear
and cold, like an invitation to definition.
But some things had become impossible. It was impossible
to waltz or to sew on buttons. We could, however,
move out of the house into a tent
with a very old doll, and nobody would stare, or wave *s'long!*

# STANDING AT A DISTANCE

We take the last off the counter and now, the counter
clear, begin. She stands to one side, her
blue sleeves indicating the moment: she's brighter
than before. He keeps steady, he may be an umpire or
the captain of a ship. They are cut-out, austere.
I think they must pass through me to endure
although I am neither ready nor
capacious.
          She goes first, aware
of sloped light over chairs on the porch where
the dense continuation is a marriage. His eye
rests easily on nothing; where nothing meets.
She knows the low winter sun will touch three apples.
I am upstairs in front of a long, wood-framed glass.
The branches cast branches. He soon will appear
walking across the grass towards the dim solarium.
The white towels lift in the wind, causing triangles.

# AND SO

Since then we have taken to gazing out the window.
Bricks span octaves, light
speeds up to dare the clandestine opera to begin.
It is just before day. Matilda, asleep,
dreams she is in a room among plants
and wives who say nothing but sit.
The strings suggest glass, a stroll down the beach.
A tall man enters stage left, led by the tune of the oboe.
Matilda is dancing.
                    And so the imagined world
changes the imagined world with a new set.
We tear down walls, pull nails
easily from old wood. You say:
*"I care more for the snow outdoors*
*than for your spoons, forks, and heart."*
This is a memorable winter: more than the usual
share of storms. And so Matilda wakes.
Outside it really snows harsh as desire and as
particular, its fine scrim everywhere.
We take to gazing out the window
while drips drip down the far river and its
turn out of sight. The wide view causes this account:
hovering, low, the river is still, verging on scenery.
Things come down from above, from nowhere,
the sky white and impacted where the river cuts across.
He paints from behind his back,
eliminating details as from a great distance.
This is a form of loss, a reduced portrait.
There is a dark gray recess in a dark gray recess.
There are small heaps of snow hidden from wind and sun.

# EAST RIVER BARGE

The song, invisible, prolongs, but passage is colorless
and, although we are reminded that silence is golden,
goes unnoticed. The day has its moments.
Even with the hovering of gray antecedents,
heavy with causation, we
arch back, away from the sheen of declaration to where
the wall must curve and further curve until it too
is a cloud.
        What's wrong with decoration? Why not make
these lush impressions lush, and swoon
as the green barge passes to change everything but the weather
which no longer counts? A cold wet Thursday: that's exact.
The sky is a shaft of steady fragmentation
through which the barge must pass as if forever downward to sea.
Elaborate, yes, but is it slow or fast? Silence is fast;
it quickens absence. Sooner or later it arrives, as you arrive,
caused by procedure. The clouds, the chairs, the barge
(the chairs are covered with a terrible orange), all
are objects which subside as the mind interferes
with its recourse: language causes you: you must be declared.
It rained all day without you but with a candor that is resolute.

# REYNOLDA GARDENS

For some time we thought it possible to wander,
to let our grip on the inevitable
loosen, so that we could
stroll round to a new perspective:
this formal garden open to the public.
Standing just above on the slope
it looks like madness, an invitation
to impossible choices and unbearable nearness.
Yellow, pale pink, white, scarlet,
each an aspect of itself,
each named, each immune to mimic
although the scent is of a lucid, indelible type.

A calm had come into focus,
a real but frail version of what was wanted—
not defined, framing no image—
but imagined nevertheless like the end of a sentence.
We had reached the point of arrival
when loss drops off
in a generous show of moments
for which there is no recovery.
We walked through unaware of surprise: we were it.
It had the effect of an embrace
reflected in huge, locked windows facing the gardens.

# COUNTRY EVENINGS

We had spent days, maybe months, in the hopes
the irresolute would yield alternates; had met, secretly,
to offset the density which is haphazard and unaccountable
as the sky. The insular, narrow passage of a room
had been replaced by another margin, held
in the flat gaze of a mirror image.
Had it been a parade we would have noticed something.
But things are hardly ever in place, even
the crowd of trees at the lawn's edge
leans as if to follow the light which will not land
anywhere that light falls.
                          And yet, the meadow is alert
with yellow tropes like some moments dropped on the fly.
The nights speak from themselves: splendid, aloof.
The sky disembarks, to be resumed in a particular light
we did not choose to watch. It carries towards us
a sense that we know the rest: the dim, still incipience.

# AFTER ALL

Late evening.
The delicate aspect of the day
has waited until the last minute,
leaving us with only a capacity for sadness.
Nothing specific, at least not yet.
A tune has formed around some sort of Chopin waltz
that cheats its way through melancholy.

But still, with all this gloom
a grasshopper is staring at the sun
in some garden where a young man asks:
*"Dr. Panza, where are your roses?"*
In England, for instance, where distinctions
are made.
          The dim notes play
and the dim stars shine more than usual.
Does a crowd always gather?
This very afternoon, a woman lay on the sidewalk.

# THE RELINQUISHED

A longer, unfurled space
might meander further and further from reach;
the whole concept of rooms laid
in flattened imitations: a lawn of walls,
shelves, hooks; carpets repeating patterns in
grass, keys locked in rocks, an upholstered foliage.
No reference. A cool continuum of things
easy and meaningless, an infinite peeling of paint,
a casual loss.
    This method is one of fading, of
hanging out days on end into the sun until
fabric lets go of substance and light is remnant.

# SECOND DESCENT: 1975

But the temperature dipped unexpectedly.
These inner states can be dangerous, even
with soft focus so they flare
after spending hours and hours in bed
or tucked under a log in the wet woodlands.
The toadstools are smooth and taut and sudden
although motionless, unlike
the gong or the owl.
                  What about these bricks?
What about history? Why is it far off
when it should be close, as if
someone had clipped the foreground
and our ears ring with a high-pitched note?
Perhaps because the war has ended
and emergencies sprout in strange places:
under the bed, in brown paper bags, at home.

# QUOTATIONS FROM REALITY

Perhaps none of us ever believed
contemplating the acute world would rescue us
from it. Between frequency and absence
a world is missing in action, although
one is still friends with the bride. Lying
in bed, he proposes a new form of separation
and she accepts, feeling already radiant.
The song of praise from Catalonia
is energetic and glad as your niece
who is fourteen and no longer a virgin.

Barcelona is beautiful. I know
of a beautiful girl named Gloria Barcelona.
Once I thought there were instances of magic
until a philosopher friend, now dead, said
it was pure coincidence. He pretended to be
dying of cancer, then killed himself.
An acquaintance wrote me the news on brown paper.
He left me his books, which I never got, but just
the other day you said: *"The world is all that is the case."*

Ann Lauterbach was born and grew up in Manhattan, where she studied painting at the High School of Music and Art. She graduated from the University of Wisconsin (Madison), majoring in English, and went on to graduate work at Columbia on a Woodrow Wilson Fellowship. Deciding to forgo further academic degrees, she moved to London, where she lived for seven years, working variously as an editor at Thames & Hudson, a teacher, and Director of the Literature Program at the Institute of Contemporary Arts. Returning to New York in 1974, she continued to work in art galleries until the mid-1980s, when she began to teach full-time, in the writing programs at Columbia, Princeton, Iowa, and at the City College and the Graduate Center of the City University of New York, where she was made a Distinguished Professor in 1997. She is currently Schwab Professor of Language and Literature at Bard College, where she also directs the Writing Division of the Milton Avery Graduate School of the Arts. As well as receiving Guggenheim, New York State Foundation for the Arts, and Ingram Merrill Fellowships, she was made a Fellow of the John D. and Catherine T. MacArthur Foundation in 1993. She has written extensively on art and poetics in relation to cultural value, most notably in a series of essays for the *American Poetry Review* entitled "The Night Sky." She lives in New York City and Germantown, New York.

# PENGUIN POETS